"If we are to speak with theological intelligence and Christian compassion about the nature, causes, and overcoming of evil, we must first speak of the God whom Christians confess and in whom they hope. This elegant, perceptive, and gentle book shows us why theology matters in theodicy."

—JOHN WEBSTER
FRSE, King's College

"This book addresses a timely, critically urgent, and complex topic. Daniel Castelo engages it with grace, humility, and deep understanding. Many books on theodicy read with philosophical detachment. Castelo writes as a Christian theologian fully committed to practicing discipleship. The questions he faces are no mere abstractions, but the stuff of life. Castelo knows exactly when to speak with bold clarity and when to remain reverently silent. Anyone who reads this book will do so with great profit."

—STEPHEN RANKIN
Southern Methodist University

"*Theological Theodicy* is a richly textured and accessible exception to the rule of failed theodicies. Informed by the Catholic spiritual-doctrinal tradition and fired by Pentecostal sensibilities, Castelo faces troubling questions and refuses all premature resolutions. With humility and verve, he calls for spirited, virtuous embodiment of the gospel as counter-witness to the evils of this present age."

—CHRIS GREEN
Pentecostal Theological Seminary

"Daniel Castelo guides readers through a thoughtful and insightful exploration of the problem of suffering. Castelo's approach honors the mystery of God, who cannot be fully explained and is thus inherently apophatic. His fundamental understanding of evil is a scandalous 'sickness or malady,' a condition of anti-godness. With theodicy being perhaps the most pressing issue today—not just in seminary classrooms, but in the world that feels godforsaken—Castelo's work offers a hopeful and therapeutic vision."

—ELAINE A. HEATH
Southern Methodist University

THEOLOGICAL THEODICY

Cascade Companions

The Christian theological tradition provides an embarrassment of riches: from Scripture to modern scholarship, we are blessed with a vast and complex theological inheritance. And yet this feast of traditional riches is too frequently inaccessible to the general reader.

The Cascade Companions series addresses the challenge by publishing books that combine academic rigor with broad appeal and readability. They aim to introduce nonspecialist readers to that vital storehouse of authors, documents, themes, histories, arguments, and movements that comprise this heritage with brief yet compelling volumes.

Theological Theodicy

Daniel Castelo

 CASCADE *Books* • Eugene, Oregon

THEOLOGICAL THEODICY

Cascade Companions 14

Cascade Books
An Imprint of Wipf and Stock Publishers
199 W. 8th Ave., Suite 3
Eugene, OR 97401

www.wipfandstock.com

ISBN 13: 978-1-60608-698-8

Cataloging-in-Publication data:

    Castelo, Daniel, 1978–

    Theological theodicy / Daniel Castelo.

    viii + 106 p. ; 20.5 cm. —Includes bibliographical references.

    Cascade Companions 14

    ISBN 13: 978-1-60608-698-8

    1. Theodicy. 2. Theodicy—controversial literature. I. Title. II. Series.

BT160 .C378 2012

Manufactured in the U.S.A.

Contents

Acknowledgments

This work grew out of the ferment of dialogue and discussion. For this reason, I owe my students a significant debt for the prodding and stimulation needed to pursue this task. Throughout these discussions, I have come to see that the issue of theodicy is wide and yet, all too often, approached with an insufficient theological grammar; hence, the specific approach of this book. Past students I have in mind include those who have taken the course "University Foundations 3100: Christian Theology" at Seattle Pacific University. Therein, many of these matters have been considered, and some of the most lively exchanges in past sections of this course occurred during the segment related to evil and suffering.

I have also tested these ideas with a number of church families around the Puget Sound, including First Free Methodist of Seattle, Mercer Island Presbyterian, Sammamish Presbyterian, and a family camp activity at Warm Beach Camp; thanks to the staffs of these church and para-church families for their hospitality and to the participants of the classes that I led. This book was written with such audiences in mind: passionate students of all kinds who wish to deepen their faith and understanding in light of threats to the coherence and meaningfulness of their lives. The text tries to avoid technicalities and excessive documentation, and yet, in the spirit of the Cascade Companions series, it seeks to be intellectually robust and compelling.

The writing of this book was aided by a Faculty Research Grant administered by Seattle Pacific University's Center for Scholarship and Faculty Development during the 2009–2010 academic year. Thanks to the Center's directors—first Susan VanZanten and then Margaret Diddams (as well as their helpful aid, Anna Miller)—for their support of my scholarship. In turn, the grant helped fund the assistance of my graduate assistant, Jessica Portwood, who kindly tracked down sources and read over proofs. I also wish to thank Wipf and Stock Publishers, and particularly editors Chris Spinks and Charlie Collier for their roles in allowing this work to come to print.

Finally, I would like to dedicate this work to my daughter, Kathryn Elisabeth. Often people joke that their views on original sin change when they have children (and they do!). But also, the gift of children has a way of reacquainting one with the goodness of creation and so the goodness of God. As I wrote much of this text while watching Katie play as a bustling five-year-old, I understood a bit better how a childlike disposition is anticipatory and befitting of the kingdom. Thank you, Katie, for the purity of your heart and for your jubilant skipping. You have taught me and your mother much about God and God's goodness in your short life.

ONE

Is Theodicy Possible? Is It Necessary?
Is It Helpful?

"Why?" That is the perennial and pernicious question associated with living over time. The "why" question takes a number of forms, including "Why do bad things happen to good people?"[1] and "Why did God allow this to happen?" At the core of these extended questions is the absurdity of evil. Circumstances and developments often do not make sense. Any mass tragedy or horrendous moment (and they are readily apparent to anybody who is looking) raises the question of evil's absurdity. And in a world in which parents kill their children and children kill their parents, the absurdity of evil is a pressing matter. Evil does not make sense, yet it is very real and threatening.

1. This specific framing has long been associated with Harold Kushner's *When Bad Things Happen to Good People*. He labels this question "the one which really matters" (6).

1

"THERE IS NOTHING NEW UNDER THE SUN"

The "why" question is as ancient as human thought. As soon as individuals and societies posited an account of meaningfulness, they were forced to account for absurdity. And so Epicurus asked the question that often is associated with the idea of theodicy, a question that was stated within modernity by David Hume: "Is [God] willing to prevent evil, but not able? then is he impotent. Is he able, but not willing? then is he malevolent. Is he both able and willing? whence then is evil?"[2] The idea of divinity provides people with a sense of meaning and purpose in life; the idea of evil, and so absurdity, however, presses against meaningfulness. Hence, we have the conditions for the exercise of theodicy: How to account for meaning in light of absurdity? Or in more theological terms, how to account for the existence and character of God in light of evil being in the world?

As the previous paragraph intimates, the "God question" (the existence and character of God) and the "why" question (the existence of evil and its overtures toward absurdity) are intimately related for people today. The contemporary mood is one that often finds God's existence questionable *because of* evil's existence; therefore, they may reject God altogether because evil is so prevalent in the world. Evil, however, is not something new, and many people throughout the ages have believed in a righteous and good God not simply in spite of evil's existence but in some way *because the presence and the extent of evil were not adequate enough to account for the way the world is*. To put it bluntly and coarsely, the world has always had a lot of good and a lot of bad, and people have

2. Hume, *Dialogues concerning Natural Religion*, 74.

chronicled such matters for years (even though individual misfortunes and natural disasters collectively always tend to surprise us when they occur);[3] in other words, joy, happiness, pain, and evil are nothing new.

The particular exercise of theodicy is to make sense of the absurdity of evil in light of an account of meaningfulness, the latter being framed within a theistic construct. To break down the word etymologically, "theodicy" attempts to reconcile the existence of God (*theos*) and what is right and good (*dikē*, from the word for "order," "right," or "justice") in light of the evil present in the world. Theodicy tries to tread a path between two apparently irreconcilable propositions:

- *Proposition 1—God is good and all-powerful*[4]

- *Proposition 2—There is vast evil in the world*

A plethora of possibilities have erupted from attempts to reconcile these two propositions, and, oftentimes, the reconciliation achieved has been more indicative of the times in which the resolution is pursued than the content of the propositions themselves.[5] As a rational endeavor, the practice

3. In terms of what are called natural disasters, a work that chronicles a number of historical examples is Charles Officer and Jake Page, *When the Planet Rages.* The sheer collective amnesia surrounding the fact that natural disasters are part of living on this planet says more about human cognitional limits (including forgetfulness) than it does about this world. Such limits breed a number of intellectual maladies that only complicate the theodical task (as we will note throughout this brief study).

4. Sometimes, this proposition is broken down into two claims; however, since each attribute is in reference to the divine character, I think it viable to couple both descriptors as one claim.

5. These contextual matters make certain features of the propositions lean one way rather than another; a helpful exploration of these

of theodicy demonstrates the characteristics of an account of reason operative in a given context. Stated differently, theodicy, given its identity as an intellectual pursuit, has a history; it is pursued by somebody somewhere, and those particularities matter for what ensues.

The modern thinker who coined the term "theodicy" in 1710 is Gottfried Wilhelm Leibniz. Given his location (both chronological and philosophical), Leibniz stood between the medieval endeavoring on this topic and what would become of it in late modernity. He assumed that God existed, that God was good and all-powerful, and that in the grand scheme of things, good was more prominent than evil. Leibniz's approach to God and the world was quite logical and calculated, one could even say mathematical:

> Now [God's] supreme wisdom, united to a goodness that is no less infinite, cannot but have chosen the best. For as a lesser evil is a kind of good, even so a lesser good is a kind of evil if it stands in the way of a greater good; and there would be something to correct in the actions of God if it were possible to do better. As in mathematics, when there is no maximum nor minimum, in short nothing distinguished, everything is done equally, or when that is not possible nothing at all is done: so it may be said likewise in respect of perfect wisdom, which is no less orderly than mathematics, that if there were not the best among all possible worlds, God would not have produced any.[6]

---

premises can be found in Adams, *Horrendous Evils and the Goodness of God*.

6. *Theodicy*, 128.

This kind of reasoning appears ludicrous on the surface to many today (though, ironically, the sensibilities surrounding the logic still stand).[7] According to Leibniz, an infinitely good God created this world, and given the logical necessity that this God could only create the best or most optimal world (because God would be bound by God's character to do so), this world is the best possible world that can be. The logic is distinctly "from above" (how God is) "to below" (how this world must be). In an equally shocking statement, Leibniz goes on to say, "Thus, if the smallest evil that comes to pass in the world were missing in it, it would no longer be this world; which, with nothing omitted and all allowance made, was found the best by the Creator who chose it."[8] According to this mindset, evil is necessarily part of the world that God created since God permits it, and since God would only create the "best of possible worlds," then evil functions in some way to promote the good. In the grand scheme of things, evil must serve the purposes of God; otherwise, God would not allow it.[9]

This way of framing theodicy is the culmination of patterns of thought that reigned throughout premodern embodiments of Western civilization. In such contexts, the existence of God was largely a "given," making theodicy a

7. What I mean by this parenthetical expression is that theodicy is sometimes pursued (and even decried!) without taking into account the "crisis of legitimacy" the Enlightenment posed to it (see Surin, "Theodicy?" 229). Put another way, we want a theodical explanation in a culture that will not tolerate one, making the theodical task, as it is typically construed, a precarious and deeply unsatisfying endeavor.

8. *Theodicy*, 128–29.

9. In this vein, Leibniz uses a number of examples from experience, including that we do not know peace without conflict, that suffering produces character, and so forth.

"theistic" endeavor. Negotiated matters were God's character, God's purposes in the world, and how the world (including humans) came to be and function. Because of this orienting framework, Proposition 2 tended to be delimited or circumscribed (usually through abstraction) in light of the unquestionable implications of Proposition 1. Claims were made like those of Leibniz in which God does not cause but permits and so uses evil to accomplish God's purposes, thereby linking evil with good (and so God) in some necessary (albeit qualified) way.

Such reasoning secured at least the following claims. First, it excused God's direct involvement as the cause of evil, while at the same time it affirmed God's role as the cosmic orderer of all things. In this way, God's goodness and providence would not be compromised. By dismissing God as a direct cause of evil, this scheme keeps God's character unsullied, yet God still retains control of an increasingly intelligible world. Second, the traditional (at least since Augustine) account of evil as an "a-thing" or a "nothing" would mean that its source would have to come from something other than God; the blame would be directed to the created order and the faulty exercise of its self-determination or free will.[10] Traditionally, vast theological accounts have been developed within Christianity

10. The proposals stemming from this vantage point are sometimes subsumed under the nomenclature of the "free will defense." Many have been associated with this option or variations of it, including Alvin Plantinga. Although the present work tends to this kind of framing when moral agents are involved, one cannot help recognizing alongside Hauerwas that even alternatives that lean this way may overstep propriety (*God, Medicine, and Suffering*, 73 and 78). In other words, whatever proposals on offer regarding the nature, extent, and shape of evil (including this very work) are provisional at best, largely because they are derived and offered *within* the problematic conditions they seek to consider.

to account for this faulty exercise of self-determination, and usually these efforts are considered under the rubric of "the fall." Within such doctrinal speculation the doctrine of original sin gained legitimacy in the West (again, largely because of Augustine), and by its logic, the non-viability of the category of the "innocent sufferer" arose.[11] To reiterate, the logic was to move from Proposition 1 to Proposition 2. When pursued in premodernity, theodicy began with the former and moved to outnarrate and even domesticate the latter.

A Modern Shift

With the onset of modernity, however, certain assumptions about what is possible, expected, and desirable in theodical reflection changed dramatically. The turn is often elaborated in terms of a natural disaster familiar enough to our own setting, namely, an overwhelming and shocking earthquake, this one taking place in Lisbon, the capital city of Portugal, on All Saints' Day (November 1) in 1755. The event took a toll on the collective consciousness of Europe,[12] specifically in philosophical and theological ways. (After all, many people were at church at the time of the quakes.) The mix of disaster with religious observance helped raise the theological stakes. Was God's wrath behind the earthquake? What does one

11. For a treatment and rejection of this conclusion, see Thiel, *God, Evil, and Innocent Suffering.*

12. Part of its influence rests on its sheer force: three successive shocks (9:50 am, 10:00 am, and 12:00 pm) with the first having a magnitude of 9.0 on the Richter scale and lasting six to seven minutes. All of Lisbon's major buildings, including churches and palaces, were destroyed, not only because of the earthquakes but also because of the massive tsunami that ensued (see Officer and Page, *When the Planet Rages,* 50–51).

do with the notion of providence? For all the optimism that was circulating before the quake (including the *tout est bien* ethos espoused by Alexander Pope, Lord Shaftesbury, Lord Bolingbroke, Jean-Jacques Rousseau, and others, as well as the "best of possible worlds" ideas of Leibniz), a skeptical realism ("there is evil upon the earth") emerged as typified by Voltaire's *Poem upon the Lisbon Disaster* and its "Author's Preface." Part of the difficulty for Voltaire rests in the insulting nature of saying "whatever is, is right" to those who are suffering; his charge demonstrates "pastoral sensitivity" because he points to the impropriety and impossibility surrounding the task of "explaining the nature of moral and physical evil,"[13] particularly at moments of extreme and harsh suffering. Voltaire and others, provoked in part by Lisbon, began to react to the prevalent optimistic fatalism (a kind of warped account of divine providence) of early eighteenth-century authors, and, consequentially, features of Western theology came under fire.

Therefore, a shift began to take place, and it turned out to be the reverse of premodern forms and sensibilities: Rather than assuming Proposition 1 (the existence of a good and all-powerful God) so that Proposition 2 would somehow be problematized or limited, modern theodicists have usually assumed Proposition 2 (the existence of vast evil) as a nonnegotiable premise that calls into question Proposition 1. In the modern, increasingly demythologized world, all could agree that evil existed, and so Western culture began to question the specific character of God and even God's very existence *because of the nature of the world in which we find ourselves*, one that could involve so much suffering, pain, and

13. Voltaire, "Author's Preface to the Lisbon Earthquake," 7.

collective and individual horrors.[14] Ironically, theodicy, as it shifted in modernity, became a rationally legitimating warrant for atheism.[15]

INTRODUCING IVAN KARAMAZOV

Within theological literature, the oft-cited adumbration of this sensibility is a particular fraternal exchange between Alyosha and Ivan in Fyodor Dostoevsky's *The Brothers Karamazov*. The interaction takes place at a tavern immediately after Ivan talks about his complicated love life. Ivan goes on to ask what kind of chatter befits an encounter between Russian boys at a local tavern, and the topic of "universal questions" comes up, particularly the existence of God (no small matter to Alyosha, as he is a monk). Ivan begins by affirming that he accepts God; he may not understand God, but he accepts God, "not only willingly, but moreover [he] also [accepts] his wisdom and his purpose."[16] Ivan Karamazov cannot give up on the notion of God, for he has "a childlike conviction that the sufferings will be healed and smoothed over, that the whole offensive comedy of human contradictions will disappear like a pitiful mirage" because at world's end, "there will occur and be revealed something so precious that it will suffice for all hearts, to allay

14. What is remarkable in these shifts is that theism alters with each cultural-philosophical iteration, including the move to a post-Christian situation (but not necessarily a post-theistic one). Eventually, such shifts make the *theos* in "theodicy" a moving target, one that appears less and less like the triune God and more like the abstract causer, orderer, and preserver of all things. Since the latter is largely an intellectual construct rather than an object of devotion, only time was needed for it to be dismissed on rational grounds.

15. This move appears to have been precipitated by David Hume.

16. *Brothers Karamazov*, 235.

all indignation, to redeem all human villainy, all bloodshed; it will suffice not only to make forgiveness possible, but also to justify everything that has happened with men."[17]

And yet, for all this belief in eventual universal harmony, Ivan cannot accept the way things are. He cannot accept the world God created. Alyosha asks him to explain, and what follows is the chapter titled "Rebellion," one of the most oft-quoted sections of modern literature within the theological academy. Ivan curiously begins the chapter with an admission: he cannot understand how it is possible to love one's neighbors. Why does he begin here? Because, it turns out, the world that Ivan cannot accept is one in which humans exist and interact in all of their capricious and cruel ways. But Ivan raises the ante by highlighting the moral atrocity of suffering children. In this case, one is talking about innocent human beings who, despite their being guiltless, suffer needlessly and horrifically. He posits several instances (in a manner that exudes a certain madness, as Alyosha observes) in which children suffer the cruel acts of humans, ones of a kind that are more morally offensive than anything animals display. Ivan mentions Turks who were reputed to have cut fetuses out of their mothers' wombs and who played with young children, making them laugh, even, before pulling the trigger on their heads. As an indictment of humanity generally, Ivan continues that Europeans, including Russians, are no better than the Turks he mentions. The torture of children is especially troubling because "it is precisely the defenselessness of these creatures that tempts the torturers, the angelic trustfulness of

17. Ibid., 235–36.

the child, who has nowhere to turn and no one to turn to—that is what enflames the vile blood of the torturer."[18]

At play in Ivan's mind is the assumption that the world exists as it does out of some kind of warped moral logic and necessity. Essentially, he is beginning with how horrible Proposition 2 really is (and the raising of specific examples contrasts with the abstraction of evil that takes place in systems like Leibniz's). As he mentions example after example of children being tortured, Ivan quips to his brother, "Can you understand why this nonsense is needed and created? Without it, they say, man could not even have lived on earth, for he would not have known good and evil."[19] Ivan presses the way the world appears to stand on absurdities, including how a child's suffering has to exist in order to guarantee something else. He wants to see retribution and justice now and not in some kind of heavenly dénouement.

So Ivan is in a difficult spot: earlier he was inclined to believe in universal harmony, but now he remarks that he does not want it if suffering and harmony necessarily go hand in hand, if the former is required by the latter. That cost, Ivan contends, is simply too high and not worth it. In one of the most famous lines of the work, Ivan remarks: "I don't want harmony, for love of mankind I don't want it. I want to remain with unrequited suffering. I'd rather remain with my unrequited suffering and my unquenched indignation, *even if I am wrong*. Besides, they have put too high a price on harmony; we can't afford to pay so much for admission. And therefore I hasten to return my ticket."[20] Summarily, suffering

18. *Brothers Karamazov*, 241.
19. Ibid., 242.
20. Ibid., 245.

is irredeemable if it plays a necessary role in constituting universal harmony.

What to make of Ivan's remarks? He affirms some notion of divinity but rejects this deity's creation. His difficulty stems from the way the world and particularly human beings are in their current cruel state. Ivan's is a species of righteous anger, not simply directed to the way things are but also to the way people justify such arrangements. He simply cannot understand the purpose of suffering, and so he feels he cannot participate in arrangements that seek to justify it. As Richard Bauckham summarizes the matter, Ivan is

> against any eschatological theodicy of the kind which justifies suffering as the price to be paid for the achievement of some eschatological purpose of God in the future, when it will be seen to have been worth the price. But it is an argument which is valid against any theodicy which explains suffering as necessary to the divine purpose, and so against the most popular types of modern theodicy: that suffering is the calculated risk God took when he created free creatures, that suffering is an inevitable part of an evolutionary natural world, that suffering has an educative role as part of "soul-making" which is the purpose of this world.[21]

According to this "rebellion," no justification for such losses exists, neither a temporal nor an eternal one. Ivan does not give up on an idea of God, but, if pressed, this line of questioning and thinking can lead to a kind of "holy atheism" or,

---

21. Bauckham, "Theodicy from Ivan Karamazov to Moltmann," 84. With the reference to "soul-making," Bauckham is directly referencing models such as John Hick's "Irenaean theodicy."

to put it in Ernst Bloch's words, an "atheism for God's sake."[22] This kind of atheism would say that given the degree and extent of evil in the world, God is without excuse on God's own terms (namely, goodness and power). Sometimes this species of atheism is called "protest atheism," one in which belief in God is rejected on the basis of the epistemic and moral needs associated with one's sense of justice, goodness, righteousness, and the like.[23] With this kind of conclusion, the shift in theodical sensibilities is drastic: A pressing question becomes, "How could a god exist who is both good and all-powerful if this god does not do anything about a suffering child's tears?" Proposition 2 now trumps Proposition 1. Many of us know "Ivan types" in our own lives; they question the goodness and power of God because of the evil in the world, and some of these have succumbed to atheism as a result.

Ivan's remarks rest on certain plausibility structures. He can say what he says only because his words and thoughts depend on a species of intelligibility that makes them possible. In other words, Ivan is a product of his times, and he is speaking to an audience in terms they share. Assumptions are at play. One assumption is that Ivan believes he can step out of his own particularity and embeddedness and analyze the universe from his point of view. He assumes a place of omniscience, a location in which he can think of himself outside of the world in order to judge it. Can humans actually do this? Since modernity, many have thought so, but this reasoning,

22. This quote has been made popular within theological circles because of the work of Jürgen Moltmann; see *Crucified God*, 252.

23. For more on this kind of atheism, see Willis, *Theism, Atheism, and the Doctrine of the Trinity*, ch. 4.

when pressed, demonstrates both hubris *and* illogicality on epistemic and moral grounds.

Ivan's perspective is only possible within the epistemological conditions he has received from modernity; in this sense, he is more like Leibniz than he would like to admit because he assumes much of what Leibniz takes for granted in order to dismiss projects like Leibniz's. Rather than assuming that he does not know enough to make an unqualifiedly true judgment of 1) how things are, 2) what justice is, and 3) how things will be, Ivan extracts his perspective from its context so as to make it (falsely) eternal. He assumes a divine vantage point that he cannot possibly inhabit. In fact, he believes his gaze of the valley is even greater than what God has since he calls into question God's handiwork. When placed in light of the horizon of eternity, Ivan's claims are ludicrous, to say the least, in that they are temporally, particularly, and finitely limited, and yet they are persuasive only if they assume for themselves eternality, universality, and omniscience.[24]

Second, what Ivan is pushing in his line of inquiry is the moral question, and yet of all people, Ivan cannot pursue this matter too far in that he has a number of moral failures himself to speak of (as we all do); therefore, his views border on the hypocritical or at least they draw attention away from the moral gravity with which he can speak. (Let's not forget: Ivan is not speaking on the battlefield or in the hospital ward

24. As Hart remarks: "Unless one can see the beginning and end of all things, unless one possesses a divine, eternal vantage upon all of time, unless one knows the precise nature of the relation between divine and created freedom, unless indeed one can fathom *infinite* wisdom, one can draw no conclusions from finite experience regarding the coincidence in God of omnipotence and perfect goodness" (*Doors of the Sea*, 13–14).

but at a tavern, perhaps over some drinks!)[25] Ivan's critique may point to pressing considerations about God's justice, but Ivan most likely is just as much a part of the problem as the solution. After all, Ivan may renounce his right for a ticket, but—if there is such a thing as a "ticket"—who says that he deserves one or even if he will get one? More directly: Is it not the case that often the diatribes against God in the name of justice have a way of concealing and drawing attention away from the ways in which humans promote injustice?[26] Let us recall that in the cases Ivan raises, *humans* (not God) were torturing and killing children.

Although more will be said of Ivan below, one can see that Ivan is pressing Voltaire's point. Both remarks are "pastoral"

25. Hauerwas's remarks concerning books that engage "the problem of evil" appear apropos to the case of Ivan: "They seldom raise the question of who has the right to ask the question and from what set of propositions. Sitting in my office reflecting on the problem of evil is more like a game than a serious activity" (*God, Medicine, and Suffering*, 1–2). Given the tone and line of inquiry Ivan sustains, it is difficult not to assume that he is playing a game with his brother Alyosha; therefore, despite what seems to be an honest charge, even alongside the recollection of horrible cases, Ivan teeters on the flippant, making his defense of the sufferer perhaps the most sinister kind of all: a cheapening of suffering that operates with a pretense of seriousness.

26. This charge and its gravity are on display in Albert Camus's *The Rebel*, and Bauckham is right to align Ivan's "rebellion" with its outcomes and consequences on display in the aftermath of World War II. Remember: Dostoevsky wrote his novel at the end of the nineteenth century; somehow, the spirit of Ivan, so indicative of the mood of modernity, did not lead to greater justice in the twentieth; in fact, quite the contrary happened, leading Bauckham to recognize in Camus that Ivan's rebellion undermined its own conditions of possibility. "Without God and immortality, without the immortal value of the human soul in the sight of God, concludes Ivan in a key sentence of the book, 'everything is permitted'" (Bauckham, "Theodicy from Ivan Karamazov to Moltmann," 86).

in a sense because they recognize that theodicy, as construed by systematic brokers of Propositions 1 and 2 in premodernity and early modernity, is rationally impossible and morally deplorable. Given all the horrors we on the contemporary scene have come to witness over just the last few years, it is difficult to escape the sensibility that the search to explain (and whatever comes out of that endeavoring) is not enough. When people are dying and hurting, syllogisms and formulas do not help.

Nevertheless, can we stop simply with the affirmation that "evil is on the earth" and that this world, particularly humanity, is thoroughly warped? Does an honest engagement with Proposition 2, one that resists abstraction and pays attention to people's faces, stories, and lives, necessarily lead to the rejection of Proposition 1, that God exists and that this God's character is righteous?

THE BANKRUPTCY OF THEODICY

In many ways, Propositions 1 and 2 are not viable in the way they have been pursued in theodical projects. On the one hand, the affirmation of a good and all-powerful God is an affirmation that Christians necessarily hold, but one would be wise to stop and ask, Why these attributes in particular, and how are they being defined? For instance, does "good" here mean "nice"? If so, then one has essentially sentimentalized God, and such a god is inconsonant with the biblical depiction of God. After all, believers are not only called to love God but in a very real and pressing way to fear God as well.[27]

---

27. For more on the topic of fearing God and its theological importance, see Castelo, "Fear of the Lord as Theological Method."

A "nice" god is not the God of Abraham, Isaac, and Jacob, the God revealed and on display in the life of Jesus of Nazareth.

What about "all-powerful"? This attribute is deeply problematic, especially if it is hailed as a nonnegotiable requirement for theodical reflection. Why not loving, merciful, just, or any other perfections of the divine life? Furthermore—and this line of inquiry is even more telling of the difficulty—what account of power is assumed when God is said to be "all-powerful"? Is this the power of a CEO, one of calling all the shots and managing (perhaps even micromanaging) everything? Or is it the power of the "Lamb slain from the foundation of the world" (Rev 13:8, author's translation)? The privileging of God's omnipotence in theodical (and even soteriological) reflection is a non-starter. If God can prevent all evil things from happening, and if doing so is a precondition for God's goodness, then there is nowhere to go from here, given our experience.[28] Again, rather than talking in abstractions, one would be well served by a dose of concretization: God created the cosmos; God could do any number of things but God has chosen to do some particular things (with Israel and through Jesus); and this cosmos, as we know it, is not the "very good" cosmos of Genesis 1, but the cosmos of Genesis 3 onward. All of this is to say that if what is at stake in Proposition 1 is the character of God, then the understanding of the divine character has to be shaped and formed by the story of this God with Israel as it is accented in the life of Jesus. Within this story, omnipotence (as it is usually negotiated) is not a key attribute by which to register and understand YHWH or one that best describes the person and work of Jesus. Why then is

28. See Hall, *God and Human Suffering*, 97–98.

omnipotence one of the chief attributes to talk about God in theodical reflection, and why does its connotative spectrum revolve more around "control" than (to take but one example) "patience" or (to use the older phrasing) "longsuffering"?

Equally problematic is the way Proposition 2 is negotiated in our more proximate context. Ivan seems to conclude in the exchange that suffering and pain are ultimately irredeemable. Is this postulate obvious? Can tragic events and horrors never be made right? One should wrestle with these questions because flippant answers will not do. Again, explanation is not helpful here, but then, neither is nihilism. Yes, "solutions" have a violence all their own, but so does a resignation that involves a kind of captivity, one that suggests that what has befallen us must always exercise a dominion over us. Whereas Proposition 1 potentially offers a "cheap hope," Proposition 2 potentially renders a "costly fatalism," and both, when they reach these conclusions, collapse under the pressures of a society that has no guiding moral framework, no agreed upon account of the good, the true, and the beautiful.[29]

Theodicy, as often pursued in the contemporary, popular scene, ultimately fails because the nature of its considerations is not so much metaphysical as moral. But if the matter is moral, then, for Christians, it also has to be theological; and if theological, then trinitarian; and if trinitarian, then christological and pneumatological; and if christological and pneumatological, then ecclesial; and if ecclesial, then eschatological. Unfortunately, most Christian theodicists do not go down this route of dogmatic loci; rather, they persist in their explorations as if the terms and conceptualities they use are

29. A work that exposes this contemporary condition is Long, *Goodness of God*.

self-evident and self-justifying. In turn, they run the risk of promoting construals, trajectories, problems, and tentative answers that are captive to their operational (and perhaps even atheological) assumptions, a move that presses the question once again: "And whence the assumptions?"

MOVING FORWARD

So, what to do? What can and ought be said about God and evil? What follows is an account that is self-understood as a *theological* reconstruction and counterproposal to what is often considered to be a philosophical concern. As a general philosophical endeavor, theodicy falls short because the key terms in question, "God" and "evil," are often insufficiently developed or nuanced because they are usually devoid of a theologically substantiating context. For instance, which god is in question? If one takes notice of how the god of modern theodical reflection is portrayed, this god tends to be the one associated with deism.[30] As Ken Surin remarks, "Virtually every contemporary discussion of the theodicy-question is premised . . . on an understanding of 'God' overwhelmingly constrained by the principles of *seventeenth and eighteenth century* philosophical theism."[31] The God of Israel, the Father

---

30. Although this text has been ambiguous so far in the use of this word, now is the time to be more exact: The term "god" will be capitalized when the triune God of Christian confession is understood; all other rival conceptualities will be considered with the lowercase form.

31. *Theology and the Problem of Evil*, 4. And this archaeological declaration has consequences for what follows, as Alasdair MacIntyre notes: "The God in whom the nineteenth and early twentieth centuries came to disbelieve had been invented only in the seventeenth century" (MacIntyre and Ricoeur, *Religious Significance of Atheism*, 14).

of Jesus Christ, is not the god of deism. These kinds of con-flations muddle the theodical enterprise from the beginning. The conception of the *theos* in "theodicy" has transitioned and changed over the years. Without any context, the term "god" could mean any number of incommensurable things.

Furthermore, which account of evil is at play? Is evil simply a "problem" that can be fixed like a mathematical or logical problem? If not, then the language of "problem" to describe evil is itself problematic. Is evil something we intui-tively know, or is it something that we have to learn to see, in part because we are its sometime victims *and* espousers? Is evil intrinsic to the knowledge and possibility of goodness, or are they (theologically) worlds apart? Would evil and death inhabit opposite sides of the supernatural–natural divide, or in some sense are evil, pain, suffering, and death tied?

And so, again: What does a theologically self-under-stood theodical proposal look like? If the language of "theo-dicy" is to persist (and I think it may),[32] then it has to begin with an account of the god in question, and not simply an intellectual account but a praxis-oriented one.[33] A revamped *theological* theodicy would begin with an affirmation of the

32. I continue to use the language of theodicy because its instantiat-ing concerns persist: how to account for meaning and absurdity. But I hope to move beyond the ways that theodicy has taken shape in the past to offer another stage in the conversation, one that recognizes the limits of past proposals and does so from the Christian way of life as it can be understood and negotiated within a particular framing of the current Western intellectual and moral climate.

33. A running theme of the present work is that theodicy, when approached as a strictly theoretical problem, is problematic for the sheer abstraction and detachment such work implies; to use Terrence W. Tilley's phrasing, theodicy is a "discourse practice which is 'impractical'" (*Evils of Theodicy*, 229), and so, given Tilley's title, potentially evil as well.

triune God as self-revealed mystery, one who is apprehended within the modality of worship. The theological category of mystery is controversial in theological work because often it is used as a convenient appeal when the logical limits of a particular conceptuality are pressed. Put colloquially, when "the going gets tough," when a question becomes a bit too pointed so that a person cannot answer it, the "mystery card" is often pulled. If the category of mystery is used in this way, then it is being abused, for the category of mystery is not the trump card one uses when the questions become too hard or pressing but rather the basis that makes possible everything else that follows.[34]

However, if one wishes to include God in some kind of sustained, reflective, worshipful manner, then one has to recognize that one is dealing with an entity who is a radically transcendent Other.[35] In a very important way, God is beyond human words, concepts, and aspirations, and yet Christians affirm that they have come to believe through the revealed-ness of this One that they come from and are returning to this God and that this God is the source of beauty and truth as well as the one true object of human delight. Christians believe they can speak truthfully but not exhaustively of God,

34. Perhaps the aversion toward "mystery" within certain theological camps is a reflection of this abuse, but the alternatives can be equally if not more problematic. If one peruses Protestant introductory theology texts, one of the first chapters tends to be on "revelation," whereas many Orthodox primers tend to start off with "God as mystery." Such variance in starting points inevitably shapes what follows, both in terms of content as well as desiderata.

35. This lesson is one that Christian contemporaries ought to learn from the revered witnesses of old, especially those in the apophatic/mystical camp.

and the latter limit has to be recognized humbly, prayerfully, and fearfully, for if it is not, then projects of self-deception and self-projection are always threats. Theodicy can very easily degenerate into an activity of futility, self-delusion, and arrogance.

The only factor that makes talk of God truthful is the degree to which it depends on God for its possibility and vibrancy, and this detail is what makes the qualification of mystery mentioned above so crucial: God is a mystery who has in turn revealed Godself to humanity so that humanity could have truthful knowledge of who and how this God is. This sensibility, then, would dramatically alter how theodicy is pursued, for beginning with God as self-revealed mystery would include the possibilities of worship, prayer, silence, and, yes, ignorance. Christians believe God is good and all-powerful (among many other things, as made clear in God's "history" with God's people), but those revealed features of God's character and work rest on an affirmation of God's mystery so that accounts of these divine attributes are always revisable and negotiable since any rendering of what they may mean are provisional at best. God's goodness and God's power are apprehended and witnessed; they cannot be defined exhaustively, once and for all, from the human side of the matter.

From this reality, Christians move to consider evil. True self-knowledge and knowledge of the world can only follow from truthful knowledge of God. It is only from an account of the good that an account of evil can follow, and so, it is only a truthful account of God's character and purposes that in turn can expose the gravity and extent of evil in the world. One cannot argue from evil to good; it is only from the good that one can get a sense of what evil is since the latter is a deprivation and corruption of the former. And yet, because evil is so expansive and deep within the fabric of the created order's being, some have opted to call evil a mystery as well. We have already mentioned how labeling evil a "problem" does not take evil seriously enough; now, we will say that labeling evil a "mystery" does not take God seriously enough.

Because evil is parasitic on the good, it makes little sense to subsume both evil and God, the *summum bonum* or "ultimate good," under a single term like "mystery." God is an inexhaustible, eternal, infinite mystery who by sheer grace, mercy, and love reveals Godself to the cosmos that God has created. Evil, on the other hand, is not self-deriving, not infinite, and not eternal; it is not necessary in any kind of way. In fact, Christians operate from the hope that the consequences of evil will be vanquished and no more; evil will have an answer, will be dealt with, and will be put aside at some point. Because of the vast differences between God and evil, one would do well to speak of evil in some other way than simply in terms of "mystery."

If evil is not a "problem" and not a "mystery," then how are we to describe it? Evil is most appropriately considered a malady, a corruption, or a sickness. Evil is the state or condition of being anti-God, both in terms of God's character and God's purposes, and for that very reason, it is questionable as to its long-term viability and feasibility. As the condition of being anti-God, evil is a theological problem through and through. Only in the pursuit of God-knowledge can that which is anti-God be adequately discerned and detected. Recognizing evil is vital for knowing the extent to which all of creation (including ourselves) is anti-God, but the pursuit of the knowledge of evil as an end in itself is pointless. There is nothing generative, fruitful, or ultimately satisfying about knowing evil for its own sake.

Because of these considerations, an explanation of evil, one that tries to frame it as intrinsic to the possibility of goodness,[36] is unsatisfactory, for in a way, an explanation can teeter on the verge of an intellectual justification (especially as matters capitulate increasingly to abstraction), and part of this work's matrix of sensibilities is that there is no adequate explanation or justification for the scope and degree of evil in the world. For many, this kind of open-ended approach to evil appears as an affront to God, particularly God's sovereignty or providence, and because of this worry, many seek to explain it away. Evil is an affront to God and to God's creation no doubt, but this affront has to be lived into by the one attempting theodicy. One has to plough all the way down to the scandalous nature of evil to arrive at any hope of avoiding the equally scandalous claim that evil is somehow fitting and appropriate for how the world has to be. Such measures have a way of implicating, and so discrediting, God's goodness and all that is involved with what Christians would denominate as the gospel or "good news."

The present essay is an exercise in making a case for what may and may not be said from a theologically shaped theodical point of view. The work wishes to make a case for Proposition 1 without the difficulties associated with a structure similar to Leibniz's; it also takes seriously the concerns of

36. Leibniz recognizes that explanations do not have to be exhaustive, but his proposals still move toward a kind of exhaustiveness. Furthermore, it is true that many find evil and good to be tied in an important way, that knowing the good requires a knowledge of evil, but I find that reasoning, which is also found in Leibniz, to rest on a deficient account of the good since it is marked by post-fall conditions.

Voltaire and Ivan Karamazov without moving to assume that
atheism is their natural consequence. The essay is an exercise both of speaking and remaining silent, of pursuing truth
wherever it is to be found and humbly claiming ignorance
when appropriate. Because of the sensitivity of the subject
matter and the sensibilities just pronounced, much of this
essay pivots off an account of propriety and fittingness, one
that is particularly embodied and registered in the author's
own intellectual, moral, and spiritual life. For this reason, the
inevitable constraints associated with embodied particularity,
ones that an exercise of this nature requires, may mean that
this work goes too far in some directions and not far enough
in others, given the sensibilities of its readers; but these risks
need not compromise the viability of the task. After all,
Christians are given the charge to have a readily available account for their beliefs. If this account is not somehow deeply
and in an abiding manner in conversation with what is wrong
with the world, then it is questionable the degree to which it
really can be considered "good news."

Biblical Excursus: Job

Before moving on to some dogmatic considerations necessary for this work, one would do well to reference the biblical testimony to see how it shapes and contributes to the
formulation of the theodical task as it has been pursued in
Western culture. Generally, the Bible does not offer the kinds
of explanations that theodical endeavors seek, and this lacuna
has occasioned frustration and even apostasy among some
of its readers.[37] Certainly, the Bible does not shy away from

37. A popular case within the American scene would be Bart

showing how awful the world can be (a telling moment is how quickly Genesis moves to narrate a most egregious sin, fratricide, among humanity's first siblings), and how its heroes in the faith have deep moral flaws (for example, Abraham, Moses, David, among others). But again, having come out of modernity, current-day readers of the biblical text do not find these references to be enough. Explanation is a desideratum that dies hard.[38]

The canonical text that many have turned to for the pursuit of theodical matters has been the ancient book of Job. In fact, many succumb to the temptation to see this book as a modern theodicy; however, such a reading of this wisdom book is lamentable. Yes, the book does not shy away from addressing the loss of loved ones and all kinds of hardships, including economic, physical, and others. But for one to suggest that the book of Job presents its readers with a ready-made theodicy is anachronistically to misread this text. Job deals with theodical concerns, but the book does not offer a modern theodicy per se.

David Burrell recently has made the case that the book of Job actually deconstructs theodicy rather than supports it. The thrust of his argument rests in what he depicts as three rounds of exchanges between Job and his friends. As Burrell sees the matter, the book of Job serves a very important function within the biblical canon: to call into question the logic that

Ehrman and his revealing thoughts on his own faith journey in *God's Problem*, ch. 1.

38. One could find a number of "explanations" in the Bible, but these do not advance the conversation much because of their variability and complicated generalizability; these would include divine punishment, testing, redemption, character formation, the consequence of faulty self-determination, and others.

the covenant implies a simple set of transactions, "that is, good things are in store for all who abide by the Torah, while affliction attends anyone who does not."[39] We, the readers of Job, however, know that this logic does not hold since Job is said to be "blameless and upright, one who feared God and turned away from evil" (Job 1:1).[40] If anything, the book of Job questions a kind of calculus that can be labeled a "just desserts" approach to covenantal arrangements. As Burrell notes, "Its primary function in the Hebrew canon may well be to correct 'mechanical' readings of . . . Deuteronomy that remain heedless of the graceful divine initiative the covenant embodies."[41] As Tom Wright points out, whereas Israel is depicted within the Old Testament prophetic testimony as "emphatically guilty [and so deserving of exile], the whole point of the book of Job is that Job was innocent."[42] As troubling as the opening chapters of Job may be in the depiction of the heavenly court and its exchange between "the satan" and God, what evolves is not so much a contest between Job and God but one between Job and Satan.[43] God permits what happens to Job, but in a very real sense, God does not will it (and this distinction, as fine as it is, will play a pivotal role in what follows).[44]

39. Burrell, *Deconstructing Theodicy*, 16.

40. Scripture quotes throughout this text are from the New Revised Standard Version, unless otherwise stated.

41. Burrell, *Deconstructing Theodicy*, 125.

42. Wright, *Evil and the Justice of God*, 68.

43. Ibid., 69.

44. Leibniz, too, uses the language of permission as a way to avoid speaking of God directly causing evil. The difficulty for Leibniz is that this species of permissiveness is justified on an account of goodness that requires evil for it to flourish. The current proposal on offer does not make this fatal move; on the contrary, this work suggests that the divine

The exchanges between Job and his friends show precisely the limits of theodical reflection. Job's friends are as close to modern-day theodicists as one can find within the biblical canon. Supposedly, these friends were to "console and comfort him" (Job 2:11), but as the reader soon realizes, their responses are anything but helpful. One need only take "the first round" of exchanges to see Burrell's point. First, the reader is introduced to Eliphaz the Temanite, who is in Burrell's opinion the "dogmatist." Rather than addressing Job and his plight, Eliphaz talks about God and God's ways so as to come at Job's situation from "an above" vantage point; Eliphaz understands himself to view things from "God's angle" and implies that what Job is facing is God's reprobation: "How happy is the one whom God reproves; therefore do not despise the discipline of the Almighty" (Job 5:17). Burrell labels Bildad the Shuhite "the jurist," for he raises the justice question and mentions God as the ultimate guarantor of it: "Does God pervert justice? Or does the Almighty pervert the right?" (Job 8:3). The answer is assumed to be in the negative, so the following resolution is in order: "If you will seek God and make supplication to the Almighty, if you are pure and upright, surely then he will rouse himself for you and restore to you your rightful place" (Job 8:5–6). Finally, one finds Zophar the Naamathite, whom Burrell labels the "philosopher." Zophar pushes the epistemological question to such a degree that he appears platitudinous before his friend's

---

permission is something that God will have to give an account for if it is to ever be resolved; the resolution here is God's—and only God's—to give; if humans venture to usurp God's role in this matter, they can only stammer and stumble before a hurting and dying world. A kind of moral seriousness would be significantly compromised by such an assumption and its outcomes.

plight: "Can you find out the deep things of God? Can you find out the limit of the Almighty?" (Job 11:7). This first round of exchanges demonstrates Job's friends to believe that his plight is explicable through some kind of theodical framework. His pain and suffering are deserved because God metes out punishment fittingly and justly. After all, God's justice is perfect, and God's ways are not humankind's ways.

What Burrell helps expose through his close analysis of the exchanges between Job and his friends is that the tenor and content of the latter's exchanges are of a kind that raises the theodical stakes; they push the logic that Christian believers often assume, taking as their cue the testimony of Paul many centuries later: "We know that all things work together for good for those who love God, who are called according to his purpose" (Rom 8:28).[45] In fact, the "voice from the whirlwind" repudiates Job's friends and hails Job despite (or because of?) his cries and resistances to his friends' (particularly Eliphaz's) ill-advised remarks: "My wrath is kindled against you and against your two friends; for you have not spoken of me what is right, as my servant Job has" (Job 42:7).

Fascinating in this final reproach of Job's friends is that they come under God's wrath when purportedly they were all along trying to preserve God's character in the face of Job's plight. This inclination of his friends is one toward *explanation*, a species of explanation that involves declaring (and so

45. If this passage is taken to suggest a kind of determinism that is in line with the transactional-covenant calculus that Job appears to subvert, then one ought also to recognize that the New Testament has subversions of this thinking as well, including Matthew 20 (the parable of the vineyard laborers) and Luke 13:1–5; of course, the most significant subversion of this logic is Jesus himself as portrayed in the gospel passion narratives.

assuming all along) what God's purposes are as plight and suffering unfold. With God's chastisement of Job's friends, we have here a form of divine wrath directed *against* a kind of divinely framed justification for suffering. For this reason, the book of Job serves not so much as a justification of theodicy today but rather as a biblical witness to confound the theodical endeavor overall. In other words, the book of Job pushes its readers to "learn how to speak of God in the midst of suffering."[46] The present work seeks to follow its example.

46. Gutiérrez, *On Job*, 13.

TWO

The Goodness of the Creator
(and So of the Creation)

For Christians the ultimate good, the *summum bonum*, is the triune God, the God whose life is on display with Israel and through Jesus Christ. Anything that is good, true, and beautiful rests on its source in the perichoretic triune life of God. Therefore, the theological exercise of theodicy rests on an account, specifically a *doxological* account, of this God and this God's relation to the cosmos.[1] The emphasis on doxology means that the *confession* of the triune God as Creator to that which is created is one that is undertaken in liturgical space and mode. As believers, the Creator–creation distinction is a confession of gratitude and praise, one that makes our lives, our reality, our redemption, and our hope possible.

1. I will tend to use the word "cosmos" here instead of "world" because of the difficulty of defining the latter: Sometimes "world" can mean "cosmos," but it can also imply the antitype to "church."

Given the human vantage point, the question of divinity and its relation to the cosmos is one of the most basic theological questions because humans have something at stake in such considerations. After all, humans are part of the cosmos, and how they narrate divinity's relation to it says something not only about the divinity they confess and the cosmos itself but also about humanity's understanding of their role and place upon the earth. Multiple theories exist to account for the theological difficulty of relating God and cosmos, theories that involve issues of agency, history, foreknowledge, and the like. Features of these theories are obviously speculative and empirically non-verifiable since they are construed by those who are, to use Dietrich Bonhoeffer's phrase, "in the middle" of such arrangements.[2] The admission of this specific limit should temper the speculative boldness that sometimes characterizes these endeavors. As humans who are attempting to speak about matters greater than they are, those who would venture into theodical matters can only say so much, and it can be the case that such endeavoring runs the perilous danger of going too far, making matters "clearer" than they really are, and perpetuating self-deceit through a self-purported grandeur regarding humanity's explanatory prowess.

THE GOD OF JESUS AND THE GOD OF MODERN THEODICY ARE IRRECONCILABLE

As noted in the previous chapter, the god of modern theodicy is not the God of Christian confession. The sloppy conflations that occur because of an undifferentiated use of the term and concept of "god" cannot persist if headway is to be made in

2. *Creation and Fall*, 28.

these discussions. The god of modern theodicy is said to be "good" and "all-powerful," but these two descriptors are difficult to pin down, as we have noted already. Often when the theme of creation is considered, the attribute of choice to describe this god is "all-powerful" or "sovereign," for this god's power is said to be on display through the acts of creation and ordering. If creating and ordering are the principal acts of this god in relation to the cosmos, then quite a bit from Christian confession is put to the side; what one has is the god of deism.

If the god of modern theodicy is the god of deism, what is the problem? Can Christians not accept the god of deism? After all, Christians do believe that God is the creator and orderer of all things, so why is deism not an option? Deism, as it is understood today, is a product of the Enlightenment spirit, one that sought to make reason and faith compatible. If this arrangement was to work, then faith had to be stripped of those elements that were incompatible with reason, broadly understood. Toward this end, some past espousers of deism did not think Christianity and deism to be contraries. One such example is Matthew Tindal, whose work "Christianity as Old as the Creation" (1730) assumed that Christianity and "natural religion" went hand in hand: "The Christian religion has existed from the beginning . . . God, both then and ever since, has continued to give all mankind sufficient means to know it. So that Christianity, though the name is of a later date, must be as old, and as extensive, as human nature, and as the law of our creation must have been then implanted in us by God himself."[3] For Tindal, reason and revelation are complementary, but if a conflict ever presents itself, the former

3. "Christianity as Old as the Creation," 109.

should take precedence over the latter since the law of nature and its source are perfect.[4] In a telling phrase, Tindal remarks, "Whatever is true by reason can never be false by revelation."[5]

Under such rationalistic arrangements, some broad tendencies persisted: Miracles were sometimes questioned, and dogmatic content as had developed over centuries of church tradition was put to the side or held in suspicion. More to the point, universality was the aspired goal since the exercise of reason was deemed to be a human activity irrespective of contextual considerations such as time, place, culture, and so forth. In response to questions surrounding the Trinity and the hypostatic union of Christ, Tindal remarks, "I, for my part, not understanding these orthodox paradoxes, can only at present say I do not disbelieve them; but must add that, as I am a rational creature, and God requires of me a 'reasonable service,' (Rom 12:1) I ought not, nay, I cannot have any faith which will not bear the test of reason."[6] Claims that stem from and point to definitive particularities, including features of dogmatic confession, have an uneasy place in a construct that prioritizes a very specific (and unaccommodating) account of reason—one that claims to be universally available.

Essentially, deism made sense to the Enlightenment period because the former was a product of the latter. A specific account of reason determined what was possible in god-talk, and so the god of deism was tolerable because it fit within the plausibility structures of the time. Therefore, deist claims aimed to be universal, *but they were just as particular as any other set of claims.* Another way of putting the matter is to say

4. A very similar argument is found in Leibniz as well.
5. "Christianity as Old as the Creation," 140.
6. Ibid., 150.

that the push toward universality is just as context-specific as any other assumed aim, and because this aim is toward universality, its particularity can often persist unnoticed and so unchecked. Sometimes, however, the divinity construct of an age just makes "too much" sense. Ludwig Feuerbach's persistent critique of projection stands here, as it always does when the archaeology of conceptual and linguistic patterns of theological matters are exposed in any given context. In this case, a "respectable" and "viable" god was put forth; "respectable intellectuals" of the age could continue with their assumptions while modifying faith concerns "as necessary." An account of reason reigned supreme in modernity: the order is clear, and the source of conflict resolution is obvious.

These modifications in theistic belief led to the diminishment of one feature of Christian identity that has been a stumbling block for generations, namely its scandalous particularity. Christians believe that the one true God has revealed Godself to a particular people, the lineage of Abraham, Isaac, and Jacob; this God made promises to Abraham, promises of blessing, fruitfulness, and fidelity. Typifying this promissory history is the establishment of God's covenant with this people, an arrangement in which the histories of these two entities, God and Israel, are inextricably tied. Yes, this covenant and this promise were to extend unto the nations, but they emerged within the context of particularity.

In the case of Christian faith, the particularity of the promise extended even deeper in the person of Jesus from Nazareth: Now, rather than culminating in a people's collective history, the covenant is said to be fulfilled in the life and work of a particular person. As much of a stumbling block as these levels of particularity pose to those who live and embody varying contextual locations, the particularity of Israel and Jesus is *not incidental* to the identity and reality of what they suggest about divinity and those features relating to a transcendent account of meaning and purpose (including goodness, justice, truth, beauty, and the like). The history, figures, and events matter.

The deist god, when pressed to its logical conclusions, has no history, makes no promises, does not communicate beyond the creative act, and is not pushing history forward. The deist god has no personality or character apart from what can be inductively adduced from its handiwork.[7] In fact, one can say that the deist god is crueler than the Christian God because the former is said to stand back from the fray that it has created rather than engaging its ills head on. The differences, then, are stark. The Christian God and the deist god are distinct gods. To say that these two constructs are simply speaking of the same entity is to relapse into modernist thought-forms, ones that privilege generalizibility over particularity. On what grounds can one say that these two visions are speaking of the same entity? A generalized sense

7. Although Samuel Clarke distinguishes himself from the deist position, one can note tendencies of the age in the first series of his "Boyle Lectures" (1704–1705). Here, one finds attributes that are raised about the "substance or essence of self-existent being": it is "infinite," "omnipresent," "one," "intelligent," "endued with liberty and choice," and "infinitely wise"; additionally, it has "infinite power" (45–46). In Clarke's final proposition, Proposition XII, he moves to suggest moral perfections (for example, "infinite goodness, justice, and truth"), but these are established on the basis of what befits "the supreme governor and judge of the world" (46). The morality at play here is one that pivots off an assumed necessity that is incumbent upon the "rational nature of all things." (In other words, an account of reason and nature are assumed here.)

of transcendence is not enough, and such an awareness may or may not be characteristic of the human condition.[8] The important matter here is that some intuitive sense of divinity or transcendence is an insufficient ground by which to order one's life: It runs counter to how humans construct meaning in their own lives (namely through biography and narrative, and so particularity),[9] and it does not provide an account of goodness, truth, or beauty that would mark an ever-evolving life. As David Bentley Hart has observed, no temples, no devotion, and no personal piety emit from belief in the deist god.[10] Would anybody live for it and train future generations in light of it? Would anybody die for it?[11]

If deism provides one end of a spectrum that can account for the theodical attribute of "all-powerful," the other end would be dualism. The word "dualism" means "two of something," and in theistic speech it suggests that good and evil are two equal and opposed forces that are fighting an epic battle upon the earth. Leibniz and others of the Enlightenment era found this view repulsive in that it appeared barbarous and too mythological for their tastes. More poignantly, such a view

8. The appeal to a "common experience" is again to run the risk of outnarrating others with a totalizing construct. Who is to say that experiences of "transcendence" are all about the same underlying spiritual reality? An intuition or a feeling may not stem from, nor lead to, the same source.

9. See Young, *Face to Face*, 2.

10. Hart, *Doors of the Sea*, 23.

11. The difficulty here does not rest simply on the account of the deist god but on account of this god's "followers" as well. If this god is strictly an object of reasonable devotion, this construct assumes an anthropology that depicts humans as "thinking minds" more than engaged bodies that have passions, frustrations, angsts, and joys.

could not accommodate what appeared to be the heightened sense of principled order on display in the cosmos. Once again, the mystifying force of Newton's discoveries gave these thinkers an exaggerated optimism about the degree to which the natural world could be subsumed under a theory. Such a hypertrophied sensibility could only crumble with the onset of an inexplicable phenomenon like the Lisbon earthquake.

Christians have never held to a thoroughgoing dualism, although pressures have existed to do so. In the wake of a number of heresies, Irenaeus, the revered apologist of the second century, made it a point to say that God was the source of all that is. Such a claim was made to fit with the Genesis accounts of creation, and it led to a famed principle of Christian reflection, namely *creatio ex nihilo* ("creation out of nothing"). This orientation helped secure the preeminence and primordial status that the Christian God has in relation to everything else, but it also had the concomitant effect of pressing the urgency of theodical concerns, especially the line of inquiry that would ask: "If God created all things, whence evil?" As we have already noted in this study, an inordinate elaboration of God's power has a way of diminishing the reality and scope of evil. However, it should be emphasized that the most faithful characteristic of God's primordiality is not necessarily omnipotence. Simply because God is the source and end of all things does not mean that "all-powerful" is the most faithful way to begin and sustain a discussion about God's character.

In one sense, a dualistic vision of God and evil would be very convenient for Christians: One could say that evil always was, and in the process exculpate God of any potential blame for its existence. Also, one could say that the battle and struggle are very real, thereby avoiding the taming of evil that is so repugnant to contemporary sensibilities. The gospel depiction of Jesus and his ministry is very important here: Upon reading the gospels, one cannot help coming away with at least some semi-dualistic sensibilities. After all, Jesus is tempted by Satan, he casts out demons, and he has to face religious persecution head on. The challenges, forces, and threats Jesus faces seem real, threatening, and violent. If "all-powerful" still applies here in the case of Jesus' life and ministry, then a major reconfiguration of omnipotence is required.

Dualism eases theodical pressures by offering a simple explanation (good and evil have always existed), but the convenience comes at a significant cost, one that Christians have not been able to tolerate. If good and evil are equal and opposed forces at work within the cosmos, then is hope possible? Would the outcome not be "up in the air," uncertain and undetermined, making a tragic outcome all the more possible? Without the claim of God's primordial existence to all else, Christians face the unhappy possibility that this God can be vanquished and defeated, thereby blurring the boundary between genuine hope and wishful thinking.

DOGMATIC PROPOSALS FOR A CHRISTIAN ACCOUNT OF A CREATOR GOD

Despite carrying different kinds of appeal, deism and dualism, as strictly construed, are not viable options for Christian proposals related to the triune God, yet resources are needed for Christians to make headway in the midst of theodical concerns. As we have seen with these alternative proposals, one's account of divinity makes all the difference for how one envisions the promise and prospect of theodicy.

Several remarks are in order so as to set this exercise on a specific course. Christians believe that God's relationship to the world is one of Creator to creation. If one takes Genesis 1 as a guide, then primordial reality is not the cosmos but God, the One whose existence is simply asserted rather than explained or justified ("In the beginning, God . . . "). Within such an arrangement, theodicy becomes a feature of a faith-conditioned discourse, one in which the term "God" is a name associated with a particular history, aims, and purposes. Such particularities matter because without them, any number of proposals could be devised (and usually these would exceedingly reflect the plausibility structures of the times). We have already noted how a generic or universal *theos* within the practice of theodicy leads to any number of claims that are in tension with important features of Christian confession.

A belief in a Creator God leads Christians to disallow the claim that creation competes with God or that they vie for the same space. If God is primordial reality, then everything else that is will be dependent on God. The relation of Creator–creation sets the arrangement within a particular order: first God, then everything else. What exists does so out of sheer divine gratuity. The cosmos only exists because God calls it into being and allows it to be. Because of such claims, the Creator–creation description operates from an important assumption of real difference and real distinction.

And yet, this difference is one that is thoroughly marked by relationality, and this affirmation begins with the Christian confession of the *triune* God. Repeatedly in this study, the Christian God has been referred to as triune because such a confession matters on a score of levels. The deist god and the god of dualist cosmologies are both not the Trinity. To speak and praise the triune God is to confess a particular name, and this confession is made possible and substantiated by a number of revelatory authorities, the principal of which is the person of Christ. Because Jesus is confessed as Savior and Lord, the church has been led to negotiate his identity alongside his confession of his Father and the promise of his Spirit. Although the word "trinity" is not in the Bible, the notion and construct were devised and sustained by conciliar deliberation (particularly at Nicaea in 325 and Constantinople in 381) on the basis of revelatory authorities, including the gospel testimony, the preaching of the apostles, the church's liturgical practices, and others.

Unlike past difficulties with the dogma of the Trinity, contemporary trinitarianism thrives because of a retrieval of triune confession within Western Christianity. This retrieval recognized that trinitarian thought is not sheer abstraction or a remnant of past theological and philosophical sensibilities but rather the heart of how Christians depict not only the nature but also the character of God. When Christians confess God as triune, they not only say something about how God is but also who God is.

The character on display in the life of the triune God has a number of implications for the Creator–creation distinction, but a prefatory remark is in order here. When these matters are broached, they are removed from their sources in the form of description rather than confession; therefore, many competing construals of such matters have been on offer for Christians to consider. What follows is one set of alternatives. Readers may find these proposals agreeable or difficult given the way that they have been shaped to think about God, the cosmos (including humanity), and the relation between the two. As an act of transparency, it should be noted that what follows are alternatives the author finds most compelling in light of theodical concerns. These proposals stem from respected and veritable sources within the multitiered tradition of Christian reflection, and they constitute one set among many other possibilities, but as a collection stemming from trustworthy and veritable sources, *they are no less Christian than other possibilities* that may be more common, and so appealing, to the reader.[12]

First, God did not create in order to start being relational; on the contrary, God created out of God's life, which is inherently relational. What the triune God did in creating the cosmos was not unnatural or unusual for God since within God's life God is Father, Son, Holy Spirit. *Being relational is not what God decided to be but what God has always been.* These claims are important to hold because they depict the link between Creator and creation in a certain way: the link is not strained or uncommon or fragile; rather, it is consistent with God's nature and so perduring and reliable in an important sense. God did not decide on a whim or fancy to do something entirely different. What God did in creating was consistent with what God has always been. These affirmations suggest that the creation already bears a mark of God's imprint in that it resonates with the relational quality of the divine life.

12. We tend to like, and so privilege, that which we know, but matters such as these require great care, as expressed through the recognition that they are topics that are greater than any single person's understanding or experiences.

Second, God did not have to create, but God freely created. God did not create out of necessity or deficiency. Necessity is a problematic category when talking about God because the term suggests that God has to capitulate or succumb to something else (a principle, a virtue, or even—awkwardly— God's very self). Such language works against a time-honored feature of God's life that has been postulated by theologians, namely divine simplicity, that God cannot be divided or com-partmentalized. One way of putting the matter is to say that in confessing God as "simple," one affirms that God is what God does.

Furthermore, God's motivating factors in creating were not loneliness or boredom. God did not need something or someone to love. All of these possibilities are denied outright because God in God's triune life is primordially a kind of be-ing who is marked as a kind of relating-act. Creating, then, was not a compulsion or need for God but an act of freedom and desire. God wanted to create. God did not feel compelled or pushed to create. God did not have to create. God was, is, and forever will be a kind of relating; the acts of "giving and receiving" that are in perfect harmony among the triune persons will always characterize the free life of God. For this reason, some of the early church figures called this life a kind of "dance," a "perichoresis" or a "circumincession."[13] God is inherently relational and so inherently moving and dynamic. God's life is an active, free life. God's actions are undertaken not because of the need to act in conformity to a principle or authority above God but because God's very self determines God to be in a certain kind of way.

13. The term in its Greek form is attributable to John of Damascus; see *Orthodox Faith*, I, 8.

Third, creation is a product of God's fullness of relating. If God did not have to create but freely desired to make that which is not-God, then in a very important sense creation is a sign of God's desire to extend Godself. Creation is because God is plentiful, full, and "ecstatic," the latter suggesting an intentional "spilling over" because of fullness and abundance. At this point, some early church doctors wished to employ a logical move from Aristotle, one that pivots off the dynamic of actuality and potential. Under this conceptual orientation, something is more real or authentic if it is more realized than possible, more fully being than simply potentially so. When theologically applied, this construct yields the idea of the tri-une God being *actus purus*, "pure act," with no potential realization or growth. No deficiency exists in God, and God's life is marked by a kind of "other-directedness" that in its sheer dynamism and movement seeks to share itself.

Some have found the point of God's life being marked by no need for further realization or growth to be a bit disturbing, if not unsatisfying, for if God already is "fully God" apart from creation, then would this relationship not be staid and boring? After all, are not healthy relationships marked by dynamic exchanges and growth? Does not dynamism require the idea of potential? Many faithful and God-fearing Christians are persuaded by this line of questioning and the logic that it sustains since human relationships exhibit these characteristics. The difficulty here with defining dynamism as "potential for growth" is that the definition cuts both ways: Human relationships can flourish, but they can also turn sour. Friends sometimes grow closer, but at other times they grow apart. The logic of potential is not only one that matters in terms of possibility (what may or may not happen) but also morality (what should or should not happen given the agents involved). In other words, if God were characterized by the potential for growth, God would also have the potential for degeneration, and this point matters not simply for who God is but also for how God is in relation to the creation. Within this thinking, God could fail us, God could fall short on God's own terms, and God could bail out at the end. For this reason, a dynamism that works out of an account of "fullness" rather than a "capacity for growth" (which itself assumes a baseline of deficiency) is compelling when speaking about God's role in the God–cosmos dynamic.

Fourth, this divine fullness of relating is what Christians call "love." When Christians describe God, they often begin with the term "love." Saying that "God is love," however, does not say much at all. Often, what is suggested or taken from this phrase depends on an understanding of "love"; however, the terms "God" and "is" are just as important (if not more so) for this statement's meaningfulness. We have already sharpened the precision by which one has to negotiate the word "god" since the term could mean any number of proposals. We have made a case that Christians have to operate with a clear sense of who their God is and how this God is different from other gods if they are to have any hope of making progress within theodical concerns. Part of this strategy of distinguishing this "God" would involve how this God "is," how this God leads a life, one that is both independent/distinguishable from the creation and yet intimately tied to it as well. Put simply, one can say that "God is" apart from the cosmos. In fact, the cosmos is a product of the fullness of the divine love that already is, that already characterizes the triune life.

Fifth, the divine "love" is marked by sundry characteristics that we in the Anglophone world denote with a single term. Much is made in sermons and classes that three words exist in the Greek New Testament for the English word "love," these being a friendship love (*philia*), an other-directed love (*agape*), and an erotic/desirous love (*eros*). Normally, the ideal of Christian love, the one said to be on display in Jesus' life, is *agape*, and in many ways and because of a number of scriptural warrants, a case could be made for this claim. However, one should not diminish the importance of the other two. Christ invites his disciples to enter into a friendship with him by calling them neither servants nor students but "friends" (John 15:15). But perhaps the most important, and oft-neglected, element of divine love related to the matter of the God-cosmos relationship is *eros*. The triune God *wanted* the cosmos; the Trinity *desired* it, and this desire, with its tangible expression of the cosmos's existence, suggests that all that is not-God is an expression of God's passionate love. All three features of love mentioned within the Greek language make up the divine love as it is on display in the gratuity and splendor of the cosmos.

This way of depicting the divine love, one that is self-generated within the divine life by a perfect, passionate, and beautiful "giving and receiving," is distinguishable from human love on a number of levels. Oftentimes, love is talked about in our context as something that overtakes us or that we cannot control; to use the common phrasing, we "fall" in love. A certain helplessness or randomness is implied that is not altogether premeditated but rather spontaneous ("It just happened") and maybe even short-lived ("We're not in love anymore"). The risks involved with speaking of God's love for us in this way are significant. Yes, we would like to think that the spontaneity and excitement of divine love would be similar to how human love is depicted by the culture at large, but would not the fickleness and inconsistency that often mark the experiences of human love come along with such conflations? Could God "fall out of love" with us? Could God decide at some point that, promises notwithstanding, the relationship wasn't worth it anymore? As with all God-talk, so in the case of divine love: Analogous speech (and the analogical interval that makes analogical speech useful) must be identified for what it is. In the case of the triune Christian God, the cosmos is not loved by God because God "falls in love" with it or because "God couldn't help loving the world" but because the cosmos reflects a free and self-generative divine undertaking. No accidents, happenstance, or serendipity here.

Perhaps one of the most difficult points related to maintaining the analogous nature of God-talk is the way that love is related to suffering. Many theologians circumvent or recalibrate a hyperextensive account of "all-powerful" by saying that God suffers, and the logic for doing so is the human experience of love and its tie to suffering. After all, when one loves another, one opens oneself up to the other and so makes oneself vulnerable to the other in a manner that involves exchange, growth, and development. If God loves, many say, then God suffers as well since both actions are inextricably tied: The conditions for one are the conditions for the other.

All of the previous points make perfect sense for human relationships, but do they necessarily apply to the God–cosmos relationship? Much depends on how one defines the terms at play ("love" and "suffering") and how the relationship in question (God–cosmos) is similar and different from human relationships. From what has been said so far in this work, one can see that sensibilities that heighten and soften the difference have taken place within theodical reflection. Early on, an emphasis was placed on "above to below"; among many contemporary theodicists, the sensibility is more likely "from below to above." This tension exists here as well: The statement "God loves" does and does not bear correspondences to the experience of "humans loving," and given one's sensibilities, one will move to emphasize one or the other. However, analogy is vitalized by both correspondence and difference, and dangers arise when one side overdetermines the other.

Not only is this danger potentially at work when one speaks of divine and human love but the same can be said of divine and human suffering: An analogical interval has to exist between the statements "God suffers" and "humans suffer."[14] To take the most obvious reason for affirming this point, one need only look at the phenomenon of human suffering: Oftentimes, humans "suffer" that which they cannot control, and they are at the mercy of any number of factors that are greater than they are when they do. Can the same be said of God? If individuals collapse the analogical interval on this particular point, then one has to ask if one has undertaken an anthropomorphic description (one in which God is described in human terms without any worry about the differences that could be at play; in other words, a one-to-one correspondence—God is like humans—is assumed). If

14. This topic is quite complex and requires a sustained treatment that this small book cannot offer. I have tried to work through the matter in Castelo, *The Apathetic God*. Another important contribution that draws from a number of traditions is Keating and White, eds., *Divine Impassibility and the Mystery of Human Suffering*. An eloquent adumbration of the position can be found in Young, *Face to Face*, 239.

anthropomorphism is denied, then one wonders about when it takes place (if ever) and how one would be able to identify it.

The point of this extensive foray into the consideration of the divine love particularly and the dogma of the Christian God generally is that the creation is a product and reflection of the self-generative love of the triune God. Such a claim rests on a number of commitments about the God Christians worship; they are particular claims stemming from a particular depiction of God in covenant with God's people. But the matter cannot stop with the Trinity: If the cosmos and all therein (including humans) are productions of the triune love, then this framing qualifies the creation in a very specific manner. In the language of Genesis 1, what God saw in the cosmos was good; it was very good.

THE GOODNESS OF THE CREATION

The creation is good because its source is good. In one sense, all that is, in that it *is*, is good. To be is to be good because being is a kind of goodness. All things that are rest on the action and gratuity of God, who is the *summum bonum*. One sees this when Scripture speaks of the natural world as proclaiming God; its beauty and grandeur point to something or someone else. Many have tried to make a rational link here, to say that God's existence is proven in some fashion, but the original claim is more aesthetic and moral than rational. When creation proclaims the wonders of God, the one witnessing this proclamation can only behold this event phenomenologically. In many ways, no need or warrant exists to explain or deliberate upon it. One beholds a work of art; one also beholds the cosmological handiwork of the primordial

Artist. Beauty may be beheld and seen, but it defies systematic explanation; it can also be passed over.

Humans are part of the created order, and when God evaluates creation as good and very good, humanity is part of the mix. A key moment in the Genesis 1 narrative in which humanity's link to God is conceptually secured is with the language of being created in the "image of God" (Gen 1:27), which is often spoken of by theologians in terms of its Latin equivalent, the *imago Dei*. In two instances is humanity spoken of as being created in God's image, and in one of those the additional language of "likeness" is employed (Gen 1:26). The history of theological reflection is fraught with attempts to define what "image" means and if it is to be differentiated semantically from the term "likeness." The context of Genesis 1 does not give much by way of what these terms could mean. Perhaps the most viable option within the text itself would be the role humanity has in "exercising dominion" over the creation (Gen 1:26); in this manner, they would be doing a definitive work that is microcosmically what God does on a greater scale, namely upholding and preserving the natural world. But again, that interpretation is simply a conjecture because the link is not explicitly there; therefore, the terms "image" and "likeness" are begging for theological content, and interpreters have often been all too indulgent in filling in the gaps.

What one can gather from these moments within the scriptural testimony is that God's imprint on humanity is definitive. No other part of the creation is graced with such terminology, a distinction that in turn distinguishes humanity from the rest of creation in a vital way. Furthermore, if God is said to be inherently relational in a perichoretic interplay of perfect "giving and receiving," then logically what follows in Genesis 2 makes narrative sense. Whereas Genesis 1 emphasizes the unity of humankind in their value and dignity (both male and female are said to be created in the *imago Dei*), Genesis 2 introduces the differentiation of the sexes. Both in God and humanity can one find both a unity and a difference in relationality.

Whatever the *imago Dei* may mean, the phrasing does suggest that human life is valuable; it is good because God has said it is so. With the divine imprint significantly expressed in terms of human beings, one has to wrestle with the dignity and value that pertain to God's image-bearers on this earth. Humans are not simply expendable. They are sacred in the sense that they have been "set apart" by God in terms of reflecting God in a markedly distinct way. Christians, therefore, do not safeguard human dignity in terms of universal or individual rights. The Christian phrasing is not so much about rights as it is about receptivity and giftedness. Affirming the dignity and goodness of creation need not revert to an account of rights; rather, affirming goodness in a Christian sense can (and ought to) draw from the Creator–creation distinction.

Furthermore, human life is also inherently relational. Humans are created in relationship, both in terms of the Creator–creation interface and the sexual encounter between man and woman. Humans exist and thrive for relationship with God, one another, and within their individual selves. The ancient Hebrew notion of *shalom* suggests being at peace and in right relationship with all that is. Because humans thrive and are fruitful in relationship, some have made the link between the *imago Dei* and relationality. Whatever one makes of this pairing, without question humans require relationships in order to exist and realize their potential. It was not good that the first human was alone; that was the case in Genesis 2 as it is today.

GOODNESS UNDER A PRINCIPLE OF SELF-CONTRADICTION

The claims associated with the goodness of the cosmos and the divine imprint upon humanity may not be obvious because created order is presently in a state of significant disarray. This condition, however, is not what God originally intended. The evaluation of "good, very good" of Genesis 1 was prior to the fall in Genesis 3; therefore, it is important to recognize this transition within the biblical testimony since the decay and corruption we experience today have not always been. We at present do not know the condition of the world as depicted pre-fall. Oftentimes in these discussions, people assume that "the way things are" is "the way they have always been," but one cannot make such unqualified statements since we are "in the middle" of such conditions.

And so a subsequent differentiation is required: The creation is good to the degree that it reflects the goodness of its Creator. It may be the case that a part of this creation (humanity) exercises its agency for ill and in doing so determines itself in an anti-God fashion. That the creation can and does do so need not reflect negatively on the goodness of the Creator, nor do such conditions somehow necessarily suggest that good and evil require one another for their collective intelligibility and appropriation. What all of these precautionary claims simply point to is that creation, as we understand it through our experience, need not be the way God had originally intended it in all its features; also, the way things are is not necessarily the way they have to be or ought to be.

Of course, we know all too well that good and bad in varying degrees exist in the cosmos. Nevertheless, the point of this chapter is that something of Edenic existence continues in the present, post-fall condition of the cosmos and humanity. The *imago Dei* is still active and visible even after the fall. Certainly, one often has a hard time seeing it, either in others or in the self, but something is to be said for its continuance and perdurance through the reality ushered in with the fall. Why? *Because humans do not cease being God's creation in a post-fall situation.* Life is still a grace-tenored reality in that God continues to sustain and preserve that which is not-God, and in doing so, God grants that which is not-God a level of dignity and goodness that has to be acknowledged theologically when engaging theodical proposals.

Put bluntly, the protest atheist, with his or her operational account of the good that makes possible the charge against the existence of God, as well as all those who continue to operate and live by the law of goodness imprinted on their hearts, exist because of the longsuffering and gratuitous love of God. In fact, the vilest and most horrific humans do not cease to be God's creation, and in that regard, their capacity for goodness, although perhaps requiring a significant work by the triune God of transformation and restoration, is available since they are God's—and no one else's—creatures. For these and many other reasons, humanity, even in a post-fall state, is to be regarded as a species that has been fearfully and wonderfully made. That the divine image is tarnished, silenced, manipulated, and corrupted is another matter, but it is not in this state because of God's doing; rather, God's intent, from the beginning of creation onward, has been to extend outward the perfect reciprocity of "giving and receiving" within God's triune life. God establishes and relates to that which is from God and yet distinctly not-God.

In short, creation is good because it comes from a good Creator, and the degree that it can be evaluated as good is based on the measure with which it references its Creator. That this measure varies brings us to the reality of the following chapter: That which is not-God presently leads an existence that is deeply conflicted so that it is not only not-God but in a very real, pressing, detectable, and tragic way anti-God as well.

THREE

The Conflicted State of Creation

That which is not-God has become characterized significantly as anti-God. Within the Genesis narrative, one moves into the domain of Genesis 3 in which things start to unravel rather quickly and definitively. As the narrative portrays it, Adam and Eve are presented with two rival accounts, one from God ("eating of the tree will lead to death") and the other from the serpent ("eating of the tree will not lead to death; it will make you like God"). Adam and Eve wished to be like God, which in itself is not a bad thing; in fact, they were created to resemble or image God, as we noted with Genesis 1. However, the narrative suggests that two accounts for pursuing this end are on offer for the first humans, one from God and the other from the serpent.

Ultimately, Adam and Eve chose the serpent's account, and this decision had dire consequences. Most apparently, the two claims by God and the serpent are incompatible:

one is true and the other a lie; one leads to life and the other to death. The primordial humans from the Bible's witness chose to believe the serpent, thereby marking a lack of trust on behalf of Adam and Eve with relation to God. According to their actions, God is deemed to be less trustworthy than that which is not-God. Furthermore, Adam and Eve pursue a good ("to be like God") in a wrong way (according to the lie of the serpent), thereby corrupting both the possibilities from that course of action and themselves in the process. By seeking to be God-like in a way that is contrary to God's pronouncements, these biblically archetypal humans essentially pursued a path not of holiness but of profanity. Rather than being part of a creation that was to participate in God's very life, they pursued a false divinization process that led to a condition that was anti-God. Instead of being companions of God, humanity set itself up as a rival to God; they wished to pursue the quality of being God-like on their own terms rather than on God's. In short, they sought to possess divinity by force and sheer will instead of receiving it as a gift.

Nonviable Alternatives

Now, what to make of this turn of events? Did God create an imperfect creation by allowing it to have the capacity to reject God? Some have opted for this alternative, and in doing so, they diminish the burden of guilt associated with the direct role of humanity's rejection of God. But they press: If rejection is possible, then should not God take at least part of the blame for designing humans in such a way? Such a charge is quite quixotic, for it argues after the fact that humanity must be designed wrong because it can function wrong. As if a voluntary misapplication is the same thing as a design flaw!

As we have noted in the previous chapter, the Creator–creation distinction and dynamic are approached from a number of vantage points, some on the basis of how good and ordered the creation appears to be (one proposal in such a category being deism) and others because of how the creation is so flawed and conflicted (dualism tends to this end with its emphasis on evil being a rival force against good). Issues related to preservation and providence also make their way into these considerations. Just how involved is God in the everyday affairs of the cosmos? Does God cause everything to happen that occurs? These questions become especially difficult when one recognizes that a number of disturbing and deplorable things occur in the creation, and so God's role in relation to them becomes a significant matter to consider.

If deism and dualism are ruled out as options, sometimes a kind of determinism is chosen by people who are looking for meaning amidst the chaos. This kind of determinism operates from an assumption that "whatever happens, happens for a reason." The logic holds that these reasons may only be known by God, but, again, since God is "all-powerful," then the universe operates with some account of meaningfulness that relies on the notion that what happens does so necessarily. That being the case, all occurrences and developments have some role to play in the divine will; all that takes place is part of God's plan. One has only to figure out how what happens could fit into God's will. With these commitments, then, natural disasters and mass human tragedies require some kind of explanation. Maybe, these determinists would say, a natural disaster took place in a region at a particular time because God was punishing the people for their sins or the sins of their ancestors. The same logic has been applied to cases of genocide, mass violence, and others.

Although the biblical testimony is employed at times to make the case that such readings are scriptural, the assumptions at work in these "explanations" are difficult to sustain because they are logically faulty. The one speaking assumes revelatory access and authority to say, "God did this because of that." The ease by which some "speak for God" in these scenarios is troubling. Whereas one may want to grant "prophetic privilege" to oneself in the process, it is not altogether clear if the privilege at play is prophetic or the modern, theodical stance of omniscience, the perspective that stands above the fray and explains away the horrors others are facing. Voltaire was aware of this difficulty with the earthquake at Lisbon; when some were venturing to say that Lisbon was at fault and was being punished for its sins, Voltaire asked:

> Was then more vice in fallen Lisbon found,
> Than Paris, where voluptuous joys abound?
> Was less debauchery to London known,
> Where opulence luxurious holds her throne?[1]

In other words, if Lisbon was being punished, why Lisbon and not other places, ones that are generally regarded as more vice laden?

The difficulties associated with the rush for explanation run another way as well. It may be the case that sufferers opt to blame themselves for tragedies and difficulties despite the absence of any empirical evidence for doing so; they believe themselves to be the object of God's wrath even though they

1. "Lisbon Earthquake," 9.

do not understand why. As many have noted, people are often inclined to assume guilt rather than live in the ambiguity of chaos: It may be easier to blame oneself than to admit no reason is available for a horror or unexpected tragedy.[2] A strident determinism, then, allows people to play "the blame game," either in relation to others or themselves.

A determinism that provides its holders with the warrant to explain moments of severe and extensive suffering has the potential to be profoundly immoral. One cannot help seeing how God's rebuke of Job's friends would apply here. A determinism that claims to speak for God may be anti-God in its effects and consequences. Not only are these effects detrimental for those who are suffering (because an explanation is offered instead of tangible help) but also for those who level them; in the latter case, the self-purported prophet may be involved in a process of self-inflicted dehumanization since a commitment to "God's will and purposes" could overshadow the human sufferer before one's eyes. Or, if the "blame game" is pursued against oneself, a person can become embittered and angry toward a god who apparently is out to punish for no apparent reason. With such self-inflicted antagonism, a different kind of dehumanization is at play, one that undermines the integrity of oneself because of a flawed account of how God relates to the cosmos.

2. Another way to put the matter is Elaine Pagels's claim that people "often would rather feel guilty than helpless," and obviously, the lack of an explanation before a horror is a position of vulnerability, and so helplessness (*Adam, Eve, and the Serpent*, 146).

Reconsidering Causality

If deism, dualism, and determinism are nonviable alternatives for accounting for the conflicted state of the present creation, then what can one say? If the triune God created the cosmos in freedom and out of love, then one could plausibly move to apply this logic to that which is not-God: creation is to relate to God and itself in freedom and out of love. One sees this portrayed in the Genesis narrative in that humanity is given potential and possibility alongside limits. In this sense, agency and self-determination are at play, and if they are, then alternative—and even contradictory—possibilities present themselves. Adam and Eve were told not to eat: They should not have eaten, they could not have eaten, and yet they did.

As the Creator and as primordial reality, the triune God can be said to be the primary cause of all that is. God brought the cosmos into being, and so, in this light, God is responsible for its existence. But God brought a certain kind of cosmos into existence, and in turn, created humanity to be in a particular way. With humans, one has on display moral agents who are significantly self-determining and self-characterizing. For all the ways they are influenced, determined, and swayed, humans nevertheless assume and operate with a plausible account of choice. Examples from experience are sundry here: Irrespective of genetic endowment, lifestyle choices often tip the scales in one direction or another when it comes to health or quality of life; one may have all the ability and talent in the world, but such ability and talent have to be harnessed and disciplined over time for these to reach their optimum states.

In other words, as moral entities, humans exercise a species of causality; they can make choices to determine themselves in one way or another. The choices available may be limited, and people may be swayed in any number of ways, but choice is a significant feature of how humans understand themselves and their engagement with everything else that is. In this sense, secondary causality is at play: Humans can exercise a kind of agency because God has caused such a possibility to be so.[3] The theological distinction at play here is that between primary and secondary causality,[4] one that many observers have ignored or denied, but its affirmation is crucial. Without primary and secondary causality, people often collapse the two, making for the nonviable alternatives elaborated above. God gives the cosmos space to be. That which

3. Human freedom, then, is not incompatible with divine providence; on the contrary, because of divine providence, humans can exercise the species of freedom available to them. I am operating from a Thomistic point of view here, and one can find an exceptional elaboration of this perspective in Herbert McCabe, *God Matters*, ch. 2.

4. Although the same term "causality" is used in terms of its "primary" and "secondary" forms here, one should not press the similarity too strongly. Quite the contrary, God creates and causes in a radically different and distinct way from how humans make or cause things. As McCabe notes elsewhere, "To make is to actualise a potentiality. *To create is to produce the potentiality as well as the actuality*" (*God and Evil in the Theology of St. Thomas Aquinas*, 104; italics in original). Therefore, the act of creation is radically different from what one can possibly know within the conditions of creatureliness, and as such, the two are noncompetitive; as Kathryn Tanner notes, "This non-competitive relation between creatures and God is possible, it seems, only if God is the fecund provider of *all* that the creature is in itself; the creature in its giftedness, in its goodness, does not compete with God's gift-fullness and goodness because God is the giver of all that the creature is for the good. This relationship of total giver to total gift is possible, in turn, only if God and creatures are, so to speak, on different levels of being, and different planes of causality—something that God's transcendence implies" (*Jesus, Humanity, and the Trinity*, 3).

God creates is mysteriously something that can be labeled not-God, and its call is to flourish and participate in God.

What is deeply difficult to grasp is that God created that which is not-God in such a fashion that rejection of God's very self could ensue. In other words, that which is not-God can voluntarily choose to be anti-God. On first blush, this design may appear as a flaw, but what are the alternatives? If God would determine the creation to worship and serve Godself out of necessity, then would such actions be truly worship and devotion? According to the logic of human interaction, healthy relationships are engaged in freedom and out of love. It simply sounds out of kilter for creatures to be forced to love and worship God. Such manipulated conditions would work against the fulfillment of what seems to be most fitting when humans negotiate and foster healthy relationships among themselves.

If the triune God creates in freedom and out of love, then the expectation would seem to be that creation would return the gesture, that it would worship and behold God freely and out of love as well. But the very nature of freedom and love is that they are actions that pertain logically to agents. They are actions appropriate to self-determining subjects. Creation can and ought to behold God freely and out of love, but doing so would mean that other alternatives would be available, ones that aim to transgress the limits and conditions associated with being not-God. When creation does respond to God analogously to the way in which it was created, it can be said to be fulfilling its purpose and thriving. When it does otherwise, creation stands in a voluntarily antithetical and alienated relation to its Creator.

EVIL AND ABUSED AGENCY

This state of alienation is sometimes referred to as evil. This category often is thought to be more readily accessible than sin (the latter being a more theological term), but the two occupy much the same space. Evil is anti-good and so anti-God. Sin would include the conditions and practices associated with the faulty use of human self-determination, faulty because such usage would fail to render glory to God. Both run against God's purposes, and so both occupy the same domain or condition. Traditionally, the two have been kept separate in several ways, but upon closer inspection, they are more proximate than they may appear on first blush to the Christian onlooker.

Evil sometimes functions as a de-theologized category, one that folks no matter their theological persuasion could appeal to as a reality. The move is possible to make if an account of the good is de-theologized as well. If the good is not theological, then neither will evil be considered as such. For Christians, good is theological because God is the sole source of goodness (God in fact is the good), so evil is a theological matter to consider as well. Given a robust account of creation, evil is not a thing per se in that it was not created by God; rather, it is the faulty exercise or appropriation of a good thing, namely free will or self-determination. As some have remarked, all good things can be abused. When they are, a new situation emerges, one in which evil purposes, evil actions, and evil agents are involved. All these circumstances and emerging conditions rest on faulty self-determination. Evil is most appropriately considered the result of agents abusing their God-given freedom to be.

Many have remarked that evil is parasitic on the good and that it is a deprivation or corruption of the good, and so far this text has made that point. The difficulty with such a view is that it can be excessively abstract and conceptual. Can we simply talk about evil without taking it seriously as a phenomenon of human experience that depletes and destroys those around it? Can such lofty talk do justice to the victims of rape and abuse? Even though it is true that evil is a corruption of the good, the former cannot simply be considered as a privation or deficiency of something else. In a very serious sense, evil is capable of horrific acts, ones that take on a reality of their own in terms of their causes, effects, and vicious circularity.

For this reason, those accounts of evil that operate from a vantage point informed by real people and cases have the potential to avoid this pitfall. M. Scott Peck's *People of the Lie* is helpful in this regard in that it is an account informed by Peck's work as a practicing psychiatrist.[5] Peck considers evil individuals to be "people of the lie" because "the evil" are those who live in perpetual self-deception, denying the truth and their own conscience.[6] They cannot admit their own faults and limits and so operate out of a constant pride or narcissism, one that eventually leads to laziness and scapegoating. The latter practice is projectionist to such a degree that it would tend to inflict harm and violence upon others before admitting of its own shortcomings. In other words, evil people would rather

5. Additionally, Peck wrote as a practicing Christian, so his vantage point is explicitly theological from time to time, a characteristic that makes the work all the more compelling for theodical consideration.

6. *People of the Lie*, 66–67.

blame others (and maybe even hurt them) than acknowledge that they themselves fall short or make mistakes.

Several features of Peck's work are controversial, including one of his principal points, namely that evil is quite subtle and prevalent among those who on the surface appear ordinary. Against what appears to be intuitive, Peck does not shy away from calling individuals evil. Of course, great danger exists when one proceeds to label people, and evil is one of those descriptors that is especially difficult because the act of naming evil could itself be evil. Peck, however, believes too much is at risk if one does not discern what is evil from what is good because without doing so no hope exists for the healing of the former. Peck remarks, "The only valid reason to recognize human evil is to heal it wherever we can."[7] The task is not only related to criminals and tyrants but also to neighbors, family, and the self. That which is appropriately labeled evil, then, is something that is self-determining but also capable of being healed over time.

NATURAL DISASTERS

I have purposefully circumscribed evil quite narrowly because when one moves to consider other matters often denominated as "evil," the accuracy and possibilities surrounding such a description are significantly complicated.[8] For instance,

7. *People of the Lie*, 44.

8. Some make a distinction between "evil suffered" and "evil done." I have tried to focus on the latter first, and in what follows I will move to consider topics associated with the former. As for nomenclature, I think too much variety exists within the many topics associated with "evil suffered" to make general claims, and so I have opted to use other descriptors and to specify on a case-by-case basis.

sometimes evil is spoken of in terms of "natural evil," and the reference here is to what many call "natural disasters." When a tsunami, earthquake, or tornado strikes with all of its sheer force, causing destruction and mayhem, many assume that such phenomena are examples of the groans and labor pains of the creation (Romans 8), that evil marks not only those who exercise their agency in an anti-God fashion but characterizes the creation itself. Given the advancements of science, this reading may not be the most helpful.

In this regard, the work of Terence Fretheim is illuminative. Fretheim wishes to make a distinction between a "good creation" and a "perfect creation" in order to suggest that natural disasters, those often denominated as naturally evil, may in fact be part of God's creational purposes after all.[9] When one considers that God's creation is a chronologically progressive achievement in Genesis 1, that humans are called to "subdue" the earth in that same chapter, and that humanity is furthermore developed and sustained over the course of Genesis 2, then the "wild" features of the earth are such that what we would term "naturally evil" could be simply the outworking of geological and atmospheric patterns of the earth's development and shaping. After all, volcanic activity produces precious stones, tectonic plate shifts lead to majestic mountains, and erosion patterns can produce breathtaking valleys. When the earth works itself out in these ways, oftentimes beautiful and awe-inspiring outcomes are the result. In other words, creation was not a finished product when God created it; over time, it shifts and evolves.

When these processes take place in the middle of the ocean or in remote areas, they usually are not labeled evil.

9. See *Creation Untamed*, ch. 1.

These occurrences take on significant moral freight when the loss of human life and the destruction of human goods take place because of them. The ensuing chaos from these developments often leads to the "why" question, but as this shift demonstrates, the raising of the "why" here is very anthropocentric. Certainly, humans may exacerbate such potential loss through any number of factors—by building cities along fault lines or near volcanic mountains, polluting the environment to such a degree that global weather patterns shift, and practicing injustice so that poverty spreads and poor infrastructure is developed within certain parts of the globe—but ultimately, the planet's outworking does not necessarily discriminate one way or another.

In some ways, and Fretheim presses the point, this semi-explanation may be helpful to some people. Rather than being demonstrations of God's judgment or aberrations of the natural order, such moments are simply the way the earth was made to be. To live on this earth means to tolerate a degree of uncertainty, variability, and indeterminacy. For others, however, such remarks are not that worthwhile, especially during the heat of a crisis. After all, when people have lost their life's earnings or suffered the pain of seeing a loved one die, a response that suggests that the earth simply functions this way can be callous and hurtful. Certainly, timing, propriety, and nothing less than pastoral discernment are important whenever one goes on to talk about these matters and to evaluate them in some way.

Nevertheless, Fretheim's point is considerable if for no other reason than to suggest that the knee-jerk response of labeling these moments as naturally evil may be a bit too rushed and shortsighted. Yes, the consequences of natural disasters can be gut-wrenching and difficult, but the acts themselves are simply demonstrations of the earth's functioning. As Fretheim notes, the earth is more like a dynamic process than a fully developed product.[10] The outworking of these processes can be messy, painful, and unexpectedly harsh, but such qualities need not lead to the evaluation of such events as "evil." In some ways, the use of the category "natural evil" to describe these events is a misnomer.

SIN

Where evil and sin naturally converge is with the faulty exercise of human self-determination, and this point is where it would be helpful to expand the notions of sin. Oftentimes, sin is defined as "missing the mark," an act that is largely framed in juridical terms as the disobedience of God's law. In common parlance, such framing would constitute an objective account of sin because sin is viewed as depending on something extrinsic to the agent (particularly, an agent's act being in non/conformity to a standard); in turn, the consequences are also external to the agent (God's blessing or God's punishment). This way of defining sin is especially popular within certain Protestant circles, and it is largely thought of as being a Pauline derivation. This definition is appropriate, but it is not exhaustive on at least a couple of scores.

Yes, when individuals sin, they go against God's purposes in a voluntary manner, thereby requiring judgment for such individual acts. But if a sufficient number of individuals commit similar sinful acts over time, those acts and their consequences generate a life of their own. The objective nature of

10. *Creation Untamed*, 19.

sin is not simply one relating to persons individually missing God's mark, but such "collective misses" in turn can establish and perpetuate conditions that make it difficult for those who are not the direct perpetrators of such acts to live righteously and holy in their own lives.

One example of such an arrangement—one that can be termed "structural" or "systemic" sin—is racism.[11] People are not naturally born racists, but they are born in contexts that collectively harbor prejudiced and racist sentiments. Where do such sentiments come from? They originate because certain individuals commit similar acts over time that in turn perpetuate conditions and consequences for those who would follow such arrangements. These decisions relating to systemic power and abuse in turn shape and mold people over time, sometimes in an explicit way, but usually in a more tacit, nefarious, and subtle manner.[12] Over time, these patterns produce racist societies and contexts, and when people are born in such arrangements, they are "naturally" and inevitably shaped by such conditions. This kind of shaping is so basic and so primal that once it is brought to the fore of an individual's self-consciousness, it often requires a lifetime of struggle to check and hold at bay.

In addition to structural or systemic sin, another feature of sin is unaccounted for by the typical juridical model. Sin also has to do with the very structure and corruption of our own being. Sin is not just about falling short of an outside

11. I use the example of racism because it is a popular example of structural sin; I think the same can be said about other sins, including violence, misogyny, and greed.

12. A work that exposes this matter in structural ways, particularly for an evangelical constituency, is Michael Emerson and Christian Smith, *Divided by Faith*.

standard that we strive to match up to. Sin also affects us at the core of our being. Sometimes this view is considered the "subjective" approach to sin because rather than focusing on external concerns this alternative emphasizes how sin affects us from the inside out. According to this view, sin is bad for us. Sin destroys us from within. It goes against human flourishing and happiness; therefore, *sin is anti-God, and so anti-creation and anti-human.* Sin is the most unnatural thing there is. In a very sobering sense, sinful humans are "less than human" because they are living within a substandard state, one that is less than what they were intended to be.

These sundry sentiments about sin are a bit counterintuitive, perhaps, because oftentimes in the struggle against sin humans think that sin represents a lingering temptation to do that which is pleasurable and self-serving. Undoubtedly, sin is associated with scenarios in which "quick fixes" of pleasure and satisfaction are on display, but this understanding is at its core a deception. Christians have to operate with the conviction that sin is bad for them. If they do not, then sin is considered as a kind of good, and resistance would be all the more difficult. But sin is not a self-generating good. Quite the contrary: sin cannot sustain long-term happiness; it takes a toll on human life, as when one says that another person has led a "hard life." This perspective is highlighted through the Eastern Orthodox account of sin, one that looks at sin more as a disease or an ailment that afflicts humanity's core being and not simply their status before God.

As a corollary to what was said in the previous chapter, Christians ought to be reenchanted with just how good creation is, but they should also delve seriously into and be horrified with just how bad sin is. As has become evident throughout this essay, engaging in theodicy in a theological manner requires a reenvisioning so that things are looked at with a new perspective and urgency. Creation is good and beautiful, but often it is overlooked as such because of our busy, technologically driven, and utility-minded lives. Furthermore, sin is harmful and destructive, and yet often it is viewed otherwise because of boredom, indifference, or a general void of meaningfulness in one's life.

THE DEVIL

With the topic at hand, namely the conflicted state of God's creation, a theme has to be touched on that is not very popular today. Although an unpopular topic for most Christians and society in general, the Christian testimony throughout the ages has professed the existence of an anti-God entity, namely the devil. What to make of this entity? Much of what Christians assume about "the satan" (Hebrew, meaning "the accuser") is derived from hearsay and folk tales. The Bible itself rarely depicts this entity, and when it does, the manner is not extensive or clear.[13] Wright mentions that Satan seems "opposed not only to humankind, to Israel, and to Jesus but to creation itself."[14] He continues: "The height of the satan's aim is death. . . . The means that the satan has chosen to bring the world and humans to death is sin . . . The biblical picture of the satan is thus of a nonhuman and nondivine quasi-personal force which seems bent on attacking and destroying

13. Moments include Genesis 3 (here mentioned as "the serpent"), 1 Chronicles 21, Job, Zechariah 3 (the accuser), Daniel, and Matthew 4/ Luke 4 (the temptation of Jesus).

14. Wright, *Evil and the Justice of God*, 109.

creation in general and humankind in particular, and above all on thwarting God's project of remaking the world and human beings in and through Jesus Christ and the Holy Spirit."[15]

Given the existence of Satan and the extent of this one's work, it is important to avoid taking this one too seriously as well as too lightly.[16] How does one take Satan too seriously? One does so by assuming that he is more powerful than God, that sin, suffering, and death have the final say on the significance and meaning of existence. Humans can resist the temptations of the devil in that they have seen that it can be done through the example of Jesus. Resistance, however, is not a given, and people can also act according to evil purposes, which are more expansive than some "quasi- or sub-personal" entity. Furthermore, taking the devil too seriously is a way of not taking oneself seriously enough; in other words, the devil is an easy scapegoat for people not to take responsibility for their actions, a move that just furthers the cycle of evil.

On the other hand, one runs significant risks when one takes Satan too lightly, as when the demonic is denounced outright as myth, and evil is taken simply as a problem requiring a rational solution because its reach and grasp are only minimal. Given the indications within the New Testament witness, the condition of the world operates from a "provisional cosmic dualism"[17] that seriously threatens life and the purposes of God. If one dismisses or grows hardened to the severity and urgency of this condition, one demonstrates a

15. Wright, *Evil and the Justice of God*, 109.

16. A point Wright (*Evil and the Justice of God*, 110) takes from C. S. Lewis's *Screwtape Letters*.

17. This language is Hart's (*The Doors of the Sea*, 62).

profane ignorance of just how depraved, hurting, and lost the world currently is.

Christians live in an uneasy tension that is thoroughly eschatological: They believe that the world is mired in decay, chaos, and meaninglessness, and yet within this world God is giving rise to the firstfruits of the kingdom. The dialectic of acknowledging the severity and urgency of the battle without taking away from the decisiveness of the promised (and in some resurrection sense, actualized) victory is one that cannot be inhabited without the abiding presence and work of the Holy Spirit; it is a truly cosmic battle that has taken a distinctive turn of events with the Lamb that was slain.

Nevertheless, it is a battle that continues today, and one ought to acknowledge it as nothing less than a battle or war.[18] The forces of evil, sin, death, and, yes, the devil are rampant throughout the world. One cannot dismiss these forces as benign flaws or shortcomings. Rather, they are truly anti-God powers, and so they are anti-life and anti-human. One of the saddest features of Christian existence today is that the dire predicament of the world (which would include the state of our neighborhoods, friends, and even families) oftentimes is not attended to with the kind of zeal and mobilization that it requires. The battle and its consequences are real. Christians should be first in line to fight with dispositions and acts of truth and love.

18. Although I have some reservations about certain features of his project, I commend Gregory Boyd for titling his efforts a "trinitarian warfare theodicy" in *Satan and the Problem of Evil*. I think the tone of "warfare" sets the matter as seriously as it can be, for these are life-and-death issues.

THE PERSISTENT QUESTION: HUMAN SUFFERING

The proverbial elephant in the room in theodical discussions is not so much natural disasters, sin, or the devil per se but suffering, particularly human suffering and pain. Where does pain and suffering fit into the picture of theodicy? After all, it is usually in light of such instances that people ask the "why" question in their own lives. Sometimes atrocities and horrors happen to such a degree that people cannot theologically move on in their lives and so cannot "forgive God" for allowing such moments to happen. For this reason, suffering and pain provide much of the rationale and momentum for theodical questioning, to the degree that God's existence is often questioned in light of its surrounding pressures.

Sometimes pain and suffering are viewed as "necessary evils" to bring about growth in one's life, and the evidence for such thinking is often anecdotal. Oftentimes it is because of adversity and resistance that people rise to the occasion and become better than what they believe they would have been otherwise. "What doesn't kill you makes you stronger" is the popular phrase. Anatomically, muscles grow by tearing; at a more relational level, humans usually grow and mature more through their losses and tragedies than they do through their achievements and successes. And growth is a good thing, right? Therefore, suffering and pain are said to be somehow intrinsic to the good; without them, we would not have the impetus to grow in the good, to become wiser and more mature.

Whereas it is true that people often grow in their appreciation of the good because of their acquaintance with evil, suffering, and the like, an account of the good that requires evil and suffering so that it is even "better" is actually a deficient good. This point has been repeatedly raised in this study because of its unintuitive register within our minds. Evil, suffering, and sin are not part of the original creation; as such, they are aberrations of the intended order of things. In a post-fall condition, where evil, sin, and suffering are rampant, interrelationships between these and the good may be possible but only in a derivative kind of fashion. As David Bentley Hart reflects, "Christian thought, from the outset, denies that (in themselves) suffering, death, and evil have any ultimate value or spiritual meaning at all. It claims that they are cosmic contingencies, ontological shadows, intrinsically devoid of substance or purpose, however much God may—under the conditions of a fallen order—make them the occasions for accomplishing his good ends."[19] We have to reckon with the scandalous nature of suffering, evil, and death. After all, inherent to the phrase, "What doesn't kill you makes you stronger" is the oft-neglected possibility that "you can die." We can be overcome and overtaken by evil, sin, and suffering. All of us will die.

And it is in light of death that suffering and pain should be placed. The endgame of suffering and pain is death; suffering and pain point and lead to death. And death is at its core the denial of life. It would be highly speculative to sustain the line of inquiry of whether Adam and Eve could have died in a pre-fallen state; there is no way to know. What one can observe is that death is the denial of life, and as such, it has been deemed by Christian tradition as the primary and most determinate consequence of the fall. Death is not a good thing;

19. *Doors of the Sea*, 61.

although it may be a resting place, the cessation of suffering, and although it may be viewed as a rite of passage into eternal life, death is not something good in and of itself. In this light, suffering and pain are not good things because they anticipate death; they are signs that point to death's inevitability.

And it is this inevitability that makes life all the more difficult and perhaps raises the moral problems with suffering and pain. Humans come and go. No one is entitled to a long life; no one can entirely control or sustain all the factors that are involved in the quality of one's life. That which is not-God is enslaved within a vicious state and condition of being anti-life and so anti-God. This corruption is not just related to fallen agency or a fallen will but to a fallen body as well. Lives, bodies, organisms are wasting away. The corruption is so vast and deep that only the one who created creation could in turn restore or re-create it.[20] And the Christian belief, one tied to Jesus' resurrection, is that God has and God will.

Praxis Excursus: The Biblical Practice of Lament

Coming to terms with the fact that we will all die is not easy. In fact, in our society we push the thought of our own deaths to the fringes so that when it comes closer we are surprised by it or we deny it. Whatever the case may be, we tend to be awkward with death, and such awkwardness may result in harmless exchanges or actions, but it may also lead to gestures that instantiate pain, embitterment, and irreparable damage.

Living truthfully and genuinely implies acknowledging the reality of death, and previous epochs, ones that came

20. This phrasing is attributable to Athanasius, *On the Incarnation*, 1.

to terms with their mortality more readily than ours, have something to teach us on this score. In this respect, a biblical practice worth rehabilitating in the life of the church today is the practice of lament. Christians ought to give one another the space to recognize and to come to terms with the way the creation is disordered, chaotic, and self-destructive.

Christians have too often ignored the prominent role that lament plays within the Bible. Part of this neglect, undoubtedly, hinges on the way modern society and church life "discourage us from expressing intense feelings of sorrow or anger when we experience a significant loss in our lives."[21] Under such conditions, grief becomes very much a privatized affair, and mourners are expected to move on expeditiously and with little fuss.[22] These tendencies run counter to the reality of just how bad suffering and death are and all the grief and pain that come along with them.

Rather than fostering a denial of these realities, Israel's common life embraced them to a degree necessary so that it could be liturgically genuine and truthful about the way things are. For this reason, lament as a phenomenon made its way into Israel's scriptures, particularly the Psalms. A significant number of psalms have the theme of lament as a primary motif, thereby meriting a categorization all their own: Walter Brueggemann calls these "psalms of disorientation" in contradistinction to "psalms of orientation" and "psalms

21. Duff, "Recovering Lamentation as a Practice of the Church," 5.

22. Duff notes that these contemporary expectations stand in stark contrast to other ages; for instance, during the Victorian period, it was assumed that widows would mourn for the duration of four stages that lasted for years, with each stage being publicly identifiable through particular choices in dress ("Recovering Lamentation," 6).

of new orientation." In the case of psalms of disorientation, the psalmist is able to "call things what they are" and does so within a doxological framing, namely through addressing God. Instead of an occasion for rejecting God, the psalmist voices his complaints, fears, grief, anger, and any other emotion of duress to God.[23] Brueggemann helpfully states that addressing these matters to God is not an act of unfaithfulness but one of bold faith "because it insists that all such experiences of disorder are a proper subject for discourse with God. There is nothing out of bounds, nothing precluded or inappropriate. Everything properly belongs in this conversation of the heart. To withhold parts of life from that conversation is in fact to withhold part of life from the sovereignty of God."[24]

Such expressions, if facilitated corporately, can aid in the honesty and genuineness of communal life.[25] Rather than privatizing, and so potentially denying, the recognition of just how bad things can be, corporate lament can be a venue for healing and recovery through the public acknowledgment that circumstances can go terribly wrong. These moments can work against the self-deception that may be at the heart of an evil disposition or evil outcomes (as noted above). Such a public form of prayer would help believers lead a more authentic existence, and as such, embody a more authentic

23. Amy Platinga Pauw notes, "Psalms of lament bring before God the raw intensity of the emotions evoked by death. When we pray these psalms, we expose our emotions instead of hiding them, as some Christians do when they mistakenly imagine that God will be offended by their bitterness and outrage" ("Dying Well," 21).

24. *Message of the Psalms*, 52.

25. Duff believes that prayers of lament should have a place within the liturgy as often as prayers of confession ("Recovering Lamentation," 8–9); this suggestion appears to be on the whole quite salutary.

faith.[26] Therefore, cries of lament express but also shape an individual and a community of faith as they experience pain and despair.[27] This shaping is critical so that fellowship with God and one another becomes both the modality and hermeneutical grid for naming, recalling, and working through those moments that defy meaning. In other words, lament can be one venue for engaging the anti-God forces within the cosmos through the means that we have been given to do so, namely through Christ and within the life of the church.

26. Important to note is that lament is not simply about complaining or seeking a catharsis; it is a form of faithful, powerful prayer that calls on "God to enter into the situation and bring about change. It is not an act of disbelief or faithlessness. Quite the opposite: Lament is directed to a God who is perceived as very real and who is worthy of both faith and praise" (Swinton, "Why Me, Lord?" 130); see also Swinton, *Raging with Compassion*, ch. 5.

27. Hauerwas, *God, Medicine, and Suffering*, 82.

FOUR

God's Healing Response

One of the persistent concerns within theodical reflection, particularly when the "why" question is raised, relates to the role God does or does not play in the outworkings of the world when mass tragedies or horrific events occur. "Where is God?" is a pressing question, one to which theologically minded folks could quip, "God is everywhere." But the exchange could continue with, "Well, if so, then why doesn't God do something about it?" As mentioned earlier, our sensibilities regarding what is good, just, and beautiful are outraged at the onset of horrors and tragedies, and so we ask the question regarding the absurdity of evil, sin, suffering, and death. And yet such a charge operates from some account of the good. Interestingly enough, we are outraged by evil, suffering, and death, but we are not similarly outraged or shocked when we are beneficiaries of positive arrangements beyond our control. Usually, we don't find it troubling enough how "blessed" we are; we often simply say we are "lucky." For instance, speaking from my current context, the American lifestyle is unsustainable for the entire planet to employ: the American rate of consumption and waste, the use of energy and the like, are all impossibly available to the entire human race. And yet, outrage is normally not directed at these kinds of "luxuries" or discrepancies; rather, Americans often use the language of being blessed, lucky, or deserving of such arrangements because of their work ethic, ingenuity, religious fervor, or some other reason. The hypocrisy here is that we often ask the "why" question when things go horribly wrong; we rarely if at all ask it when things play out exceedingly (and unfairly?) in our favor.

In the midst of such brooding hypocrisy, it is difficult for humans to engage in a line of accusations against God. Who can blame God when all are guilty in varying degrees of complicity with how things are presently disfigured and wrong? Again, such actions stem from the propensity of humans to think of themselves as being located in some ahistorical, decontextualized state of omniscience. Such a situation is a fantasy, one that is both self-justifying as well as hubristic (and so idolatrous).

Nevertheless, for believers, a question lingers: If God does appear from time to time within the biblical narrative and within history to change the course of events, then why does God not apparently take a more active role in human affairs, especially in terms of curbing the degree of pain and suffering in the world? If God does provide for the lilies of the field and the birds of the air, then why did the Shoah happen? Sure, humans were involved in the latter tragedy through and through, mostly exercising their agency toward evil ends in the conditions and events that led to the killing of millions of innocents within a very concentrated amount of time, but nevertheless the persistent question remains: God obviously allows that which is not-God to persist even in its largely framed condition of being anti-God, and yet an account of God's providence would posit that God is active in the world; therefore, Why does God not act more decisively so that some of the more tragic moments in human history are avoided? What is gained by leaving humans to themselves so that they destroy one another in such a horrific fashion and to such a degree?

In some ways, this question appears similar to the questioning that a protest atheist would level, but when pressed, the two questions are possibly very different because they may stem from two very different conditions. Protest atheists as well as "rebels" like Ivan Karamazov operate from an intuitively and passionately held account of the good. In order to level their critique, these critics require an operative account of the good, and yet its basis and reach are indeterminate because these inquirers are more interested in calling out inconsistencies than taking inventory of the good's source, shape, and rationale. However, the believer who raises this line of questioning does so within the condition of faith. For this person, God is the *summum bonum*, the greatest good; God is the source of truth, justice, and life. For these reasons, this person is shocked by how horrible the world can be in its present form and wishes for God's reign and work to be more evident within the creation. The "protest" here is against how bad things are with a desire that God's kingdom be established and on display.

GOD *HAS* DONE SOMETHING: JESUS CHRIST

Where and how is God's kingdom established? In other words, where is God at work, and how is God healing and repairing the world? For Christians, the first place to turn is the person and work of Christ, for with this one, God's expression is one of identification with human plight as well as victory over it.

In terms of identifying with the human condition, one pivotal moment is Jesus' cry on the cross, often called the "cry of dereliction." The cry itself, "My God, my God, why have you forsaken me?"[1] is a lament, one found in Psalm 22. The cry is directed to God by the God-human, and the response is inconclusive in the immediate aftermath. The moment represents a significant rupture, one in which the fullness of the anti-God condition is expressed with all its accompanying anguish, pain, and rejection. God through the Son takes on creation's alienated state and lives through it to its end.

The cry of dereliction opens the possibility to frame the "why" question christologically: Why did Jesus die? Furthermore, what does it mean for Jesus to say that God has forsaken him? With a high Christology in view, what does it mean to say that God forsakes God? Equally worth registering in terms of a low Christology, what does it mean to say that God forsakes humanity? Both are vital questions because both result from the identity and condition of the crucified Jesus.

The importance and significance of the crucifixion are not so much in terms of the brutality involved with such a form of execution but in light of the identity of the one

1. See Matt 27:46 and Mark 15:34. Luke reports that Jesus said, "Father, into your hands I commend my spirit" (Luke 23:46); among other words in the Fourth Gospel, John reports Jesus as saying, "It is finished" (John 19:30).

crucified. The one crucified is the God-human, Jesus the Christ. The difficulty of the cross is due to the scandal associated with the identity of the one being crucified. Christians believe that Jesus is Israel's long-awaited Messiah, the anticipated prophet like Moses, and the coming king like David. If one takes the cosmological ruminations of the Johannine testimony into account, the Word was with God and the Word was God "in the beginning." God creates through God's Word, and God's Word is said to be the Son of God. For this reason, there has always been a link between that which is God and that which is not-God, and that has been the Word. The Word of God is the bridge between God and the cosmos. The Word brought the latter into existence and sustains it, and, as seen in the gospel testimony, the Word saves it as well.

Many have presented a number of alternative answers to the question, why did Jesus have to die? The implied necessity of his death in this question leads to a number of speculative responses that gain their appeal from different accounts of atonement theory, ones that involve a number of alternative themes like sacrificial imagery, substitutionary models, punitive-restorative accounts of justice, and the like. Those different models are complex and worth pursuing in their own right, but many have a common element: The suffering is justified because it is a means to an end, namely the salvation of the world, and so the salvation of humankind. The suffering of Christ is portrayed as something precious, his blood as something that washes clean, his pain and agony as gifts of sacrifice from a God who is willing to pay what we owe.

All of these claims have a logic of their own, but they fail to take seriously Jesus' cry of dereliction as a lament uttered by one facing the imminence of death. The value of the crucifixion is not simply that through such an event Jesus is the perfect sacrifice for us; rather, the crucifixion is a moment in which God in the flesh becomes one with us so that the threat to all of existence, namely death, is sustained by God. Jürgen Moltmann has repeatedly raised the significance of the cry at Golgotha, and such emphasis has its place. Jesus' cry of dereliction is a moment in which "God is with us" (Immanuel) even within the adversity that is involved by living within a fallen world. In other words, God came to that which is not-God in its current state of being largely anti-God and made this condition God's own. Rather than from without, God tackled the problem of creation's alienation from within.

But to understand fully how God tackles the problem of creation's state of being anti-God, the entire history of healing and repair has to be told. The disposition of God is seen when God makes garments of skin for Adam and Eve in their alienated and naked state (Gen 3:21). God continues to show this gracious and merciful disposition in the way God works with Noah and his lineage as well as with Abraham and his. God's ongoing concern to save and heal continues in the Exodus and in the call to repentance proclaimed by the prophets and prophetesses of old, and it reaches a culminating moment in the person and work of Christ. This ongoing disposition of God to not give up on creation is good news to a hurting and dying world. God's mercy and grace to heal and restore are the core elements of what constitute the gospel.

Therefore, current Christians suffer from a myopic disposition when they assume that God's saving work exclusively happens on the cross. It does not. God is *for us* in every manner in which God is *with us*. Birth, incarnation, ministry, teachings, faithful obedience amidst adversity, suffering, rejection, crucifixion, entombment, resurrection, and ascension: All of these moments within Christ's life show how God in Christ is for us. All of these indicate one movement, which has often been called an *exitus-reditus* ("exit-return") schematization. As the ancients repeatedly mentioned, God became one of us so that we could become like God. This hope is the endgame where ultimate healing and redemption take place. Such a possibility demonstrates that creation (that which is not-God and has in turn been perverted to be significantly anti-God) will one day become like God, good and very good once again and greater still than it was once before.

In light of these considerations, God is not a bystander to all the pain and suffering that exists in the world. On the contrary, in Christ God joins Godself to the hurting and the dying. Those experiences of anti-Godness are not foreign or outside of God. God is both within and beyond those instances: God identifies with them (as human) but also redeems, restores, and picks up (as God) the lowly, hurting, and the dead. Given these factors, contemporary Christians often highlight the crucifixion to the neglect of both the incarnation (God became one of us) and the resurrection (God overcame death). As believers and followers of Christ, Christ's disciples live in a reality marked by post-fall conditions, but they also see post-resurrection glimpses of healing and hope. The incarnation shows that humans are not alone, that God has not abandoned the creation because it is largely tinged by an anti-God disposition after the fall. Furthermore, the resurrection shows that creation, although still affected severely by the fall, will not be left alone to suffer the dire consequences of the fall, which have been ultimately overtaken and defeated by God's very self.

The response that Christians can offer to protest atheists and others pressing theodical matters more generally is Jesus Christ. The answer Christians can give to this predicament is an incarnate God who suffers alongside the creation as a way of restoring, redeeming, healing, and dignifying it. Such a response may not be the answer that some would hope for, because it is not a conceptual or practical eradication of evil and suffering as presently witnessed, but then again, as we explored earlier, a theodical answer is often expected within conditions where theodicy has been made impossible. To put it another way, *theodical expectation merits crucifixion*; it is our burden to carry alongside the crucified Christ.

Admitting this claim, however, does not leave one without resources in terms of elaborating the implications of a cruciform Messiah for a theological theodicy. For instance, a God who simply shows up when things really go awry and offers a quick fix from without is a cowardly and indifferent god. After all, this god would only show up to "put out fires" but would do little by way of genuinely sympathizing or engaging the conditions that led to the crisis. But a God who bears the sufferings of the world is altogether a different kind of god. With this God, power is shown in weakness; majesty is reaffirmed in humility; lordship is affirmed in lowliness; and victory is established through loss. The depiction of Christ on Golgotha shows that God is closer to the sufferer than the sufferer is to herself. And the image of the resurrected Christ, with bruises and marks to boot, is one that demonstrates a kind of hope that suggests that tragedy, loss, and pain will not have the final say in this life.

The Open Question

If God is with us in Christ and not a distant or deistic god, then what about preventative measures so that things do not reach the degree that they sometimes do? If God is active in the world within certain tragedies or working to heal and bless people along the way, then why do the more horrific and extensive instances of suffering and death exist, like systemic genocide or epidemics? That is a running question that has to be kept open for God, and God alone, to answer. This affirmation is not one stemming from arrogance or rebellion, but one coming from a fellow inquirer and fellow sufferer who does not know. Scripture does not give the church an answer to this question, and the answers the church has often come up with have been problematic at best and violent at worst. It is a species of the "why" question that is unanswerable in this life because it is a question that only God can answer, and God has not answered it (yet).[2] It is a question that many of us feel at certain times more than others as we await the redemption of our bodies, and it is a live, earnest question. The answer will most likely be startling, yet Christians believe

2. Some have tended to say that God is *unable* to do something about such matters because of a commitment to love or some other principle. This consideration continues to pivot off the assumption that sovereignty is a suitable, and maybe even primary, category for negotiating God's relationship to the cosmos. The consequence of such a commitment is to use the language of restraint, powerlessness, or inability, which I find inappropriate for describing God. In other words, I would rather remain silent than to say in a speculative manner what God cannot do in relation to healing and making right the world. Obviously, God did not prevent the Shoah or any other massive tragedy that comes to mind; rather than futilely defend God on this score, I sense that no other possibility exists outside of silence: a holy, earnest, restless silence, but a silence no less.

that it is an answer that can still conform to God's goodness, holiness, and righteousness.

Nevertheless, until that day, Christians do not need an answer in order to be faithful in their lives, nor do believers need this query satisfied in order to have a coherent account of God's character. If one abandons a feature of the divine character or belief in the existence of God altogether, on what basis can one stand? For Christians, an account of goodness, justice, truth, and beauty all rest on an account of God; without God, Christians believe, there is no truth, no meaning, and so no point to it all. The basis for the critique, lament, rebellion, or whatever other reaction a believer experiences in the face of horror is nullified if God is rejected altogether. Those who do not believe this to be a God-graced universe have to give an account on what basis they can sustain the protest; they have to be upfront as to whence and whither their account of goodness, justice, and truth stems. Christians are very clear on those registers, thereby making the Christian practices of lament and silence more coherent and transparent than the skeptic's critique, questioning, and outcry.

GOD *IS* DOING SOMETHING: THE CHURCH

God is about the business of healing and restoring the world. And we are talking about *this* world. An escapist, other-worldly orientation in which what matters is the afterlife will not do here. As Wright notes, "The question is about God's moral government of *this* world, not about the way in which we should leave this world behind and find consolation in a different one. That is the high road to Buddhism, not to biblical theology."[3] The good news proclaimed and embodied in the life and work of Jesus Christ, Son of Man and Son of God, is for this world, here and now. This claim means that God's work entails the defeat and ongoing confrontation of evil, sin, suffering, and death. In popular terminology, this divine resolution is sometimes labeled the "mission of God" or the *missio Dei*. God has decisively affirmed victory over the powers that keep the world in an anti-God state through the life, death, and resurrection of Jesus. That event was decisive for both the world's present existence and its future.

If the mission of God is to heal and restore the world, then this has to be the mission of the church as well. The church is emphasized throughout this chapter because it is this community of Christ-followers (sometimes called the body of Christ) that keeps the memory and work of the Christ-event alive in explicit, embodied form. This group of disciples retells the stories of the one from Nazareth as they are prompted by the Holy Spirit and spurred by apostolic tradition to do so. They have come to see Jesus for who he is and in turn worship him, give him thanks until the day he returns, and seek to lead lives like his. This memory and performance are sustained through preaching, teaching, the offering of the sacraments, and other activities that witness of him and his kingdom to a hurting and dying human race. The church, as Christ's body, ought to display the firstfruits of this kingdom in its common life. When a suffering world looks at the church, it ought to see hope for another way to live.

But, as we all know, the church all too often fails at living into the *missio Dei*. Sadly, the church can easily be a greater

---

3. *Evil and the Justice of God*, 70.

part of the problem than the solution; it can contribute to the sustained anti-God features of the world precisely (and insidiously) through its hypocrisy by proclaiming one thing and doing and living another. Such possibilities and all-too-common realities suggest that the church is called to join the mission of God, but that mission is not the sole property of the church. No, the *missio Dei* is precisely God's mission, and God can work both within the church (and this is quite proper, given that God called the church to be the community of disciples that bears witness to the nations of the gospel) and without the church, especially if it has aligned itself with arrangements that are more akin to anti-God forces and persuasions. This danger is on display both in the obstinacy of Israel throughout its recorded scriptural history and the stubbornness of the church throughout the years following Christ's ascension. It does not take long for God's people to worship and prioritize entities other than God. The pattern is well documented and familiar enough to those willing to be agents of memory, but the tendency continues to register and plague the nominally faithful. Such instances show that being God's people is not simply an identity marker but a reality that has to be lived into in an intentional and sustained fashion.

Out of this sense of humility and repentance, the church ought to recognize that often on the surface many non-Christians (including agnostics and atheists!) may be, by all outward appearances, more in line with God's purposes in the world—as they are proclaimed in Scripture and the testimony of the faithful throughout the ages—than particular Christian communities and individuals. Anyone who befriends a number of folks outside of the church will come to see that with regular frequency one can find non-Christians who are more respectful, more open to listening and dialogue, and maybe even more passionate for those in need than many constituting the Christian rank and file. In one sense, such empirical evidence should shame the church, leading it to take inventory as to why it is not more faithful to Christ's teachings and example. But in another very basic sense, such instances should humble the church precisely in the recognition of seeing that God's work in the world is not limited to the church. God is bigger than the church, and for this reason, God can judge and beckon the church to attend to its calling, and such chastening may come from unexpected places and persons.

Such acknowledgements radicalize the original suggestion made a couple of chapters ago in relation to the *imago Dei*. When one speaks of humans being created in the image of God, the referents do not simply include explicit God-fearers and God-lovers. No, this category extends to *all* humans, regardless of whether they claim the identity of a Christ-follower or not. If God is the ultimate good, then when humans operate in the good, they in some sense operate in conformity to their identity as God's creatures. Yes, they (as well as all humans, including Christians) are deeply conflicted because of the strictures associated with life in a post-fall condition. But such fallenness is not total, either for the believer or the pagan. Believers and pagans are creatures of God and so resemble God in varying degrees in their lives, but each has the capacity to do so because one never ceases to be a creature of God.

All of these claims have massive consequences for theodical matters. First of all, it means that the church ought to be about the business of God, namely aiding in the healing and repair of the world and joining forces with those outside the church who share such aims. Healing and repairing the world is not simply proclaiming God and seeking the salvation of souls. Souls are embodied, and bodies have needs. Jesus taught the masses but also provided for their needs in terms of giving them food, healing their diseases, and the like. It is befuddling to observe how Christians sometimes fail to recognize the material aspects of the gospel way of life. When they do recognize the gospel as extending to the whole of creation, they ought to join in efforts with others at ameliorating the plight of humanity and the earth more broadly.

When the church does this, it does so as the church, and its testimony should be directed explicitly to communicating such a justification. The claim could go something like this: "We are helping with relief efforts or protesting this matter because we are Christians." The identity is integral to the activity, for all activities are evaluated and assessed in terms of motive. The church should be open about its motive: that in engaging in such efforts it is attempting to proclaim the reign of God. Such an explicit claim is crucial to make in a sustained fashion because over time it is very easy for "the cause" or "the need" to be all-consuming. Additionally, efforts can be politicized or co-opted in unhelpful ways. The church needs to be explicit and intentional with its identity throughout so that it becomes clear to the wider, onlooking world that the church does not necessarily approve when such efforts are taken over by others for their own social or political capital. The church's explicit expression of its identity and mission also means that the church may have to seek other partners in healing and repairing the world when previous arrangements start to be co-opted or overdetermined by forces alien or antagonistic to the church's specific witness.

A PRAGMATIC THEODICY

With such emphases as healing and repairing, the vision of
theodicy being offered here is a pragmatic one. Christians
cannot offer an answer to the "why" question that will be sat-
isfactory to all interested parties. In fact, their role is not to do
so. Nowhere in Scripture is the call of discipleship associated
primarily with answering questions. Scripture does not give
us an answer to the "why" question as it is often construed,
and Christians should not be in the business of offering answers either. Rather, the call of discipleship is to reach the lost
and needy with the good news of healing and repair that Jesus
Christ proclaimed and embodied.

Given such considerations, it may be appropriate to say
that the primary Christian response to evil, sin, suffering,
and death is *not to explain but to feel for the purpose of being
moved to action.*

Explanations only do so much, and it is questionable
the degree to which explanations can be offered in given instances. Oftentimes, explanations are sought to bring some
kind of order to a chaotic situation. We readily wish to find
the culprit or underlying causes so that we can attribute the
blame necessary to continue living with the false sense of
security and safety that we (falsely) promote. But the world
is not safe, predictable, and orderly. As outlined above, evil
and its concomitant effects of pain, suffering, sin, and death
are absurd. Again, evil is not a problem beckoning a calculated and researched solution. Given the sheer abstraction
and objectivity required for their formulation, explanations
in the face of tragedy and loss can be tautologous[4]—and even

---

4. Hart, *Doors of the Sea*, 29.

turn violent in terms of violating and silencing voices and overlooking details and circumstances, all for the speedy and "necessary" establishment of "order." Any order predicated on violence is in the long-term tenuous at best.

The Bible and Christian antiquity generally have not gone about the process of simply and, presumably, exhaustively explaining evil, suffering, and death. As Stanley Hauerwas notes, early Christians opted to avoid explanation in order to choose practices and communal forms of life that could create support and means to move on in the midst of suffering; for this reason, "Suffering was not a metaphysical problem needing a solution but a practical challenge requiring a response."[5]

In light of the epistemic uncertainties involved as well as the potential for violence that explanations may engender, it is deeply problematic when Christians engage in "this-is-that" reasoning. Such reasoning, again, operates from a level of omniscience that is highly problematic. Some take on the mantle of the prophets of old and believe that they can say that this disaster or this catastrophe is the judgment of God, which God is leveling because of the collective guilt of a group or society. These kinds of outbursts reek of projection. Not only is this activity a misappropriation of the prophetic testimony, but it also has a way of working against the viability of the gospel in the public domain. Christians run the risk of a credibility crisis when they engage in "this-is-that" reasoning, but they also pose a danger to themselves, a self-hardening disposition that has at its core the tendency to step back from horrors and to analyze and explain them rather than to feel compassion, love, and sadness. As noted earlier in this study,

5. Hauerwas, *God, Medicine, and Suffering*, 51.

theodical explanations are violent to others but also to the self promulgating them.

What is missed often in the activity of offering explanations is that reactions to suffering, pain, loss, evil, and death are moral activities. Such reactions affect others and the self in deeply profound ways because such instances cut to the core of the significance of life and what it means to be human. That is why pain and suffering have the capacity for shaping us in such profound ways, for these conditions cut through the myths we perpetuate about ourselves in order to force us to come to grips with our humanity, our mortality, and our limits.[6] Theodical endeavoring generally runs the risk of dehumanizing the self and others when sustained with the cool objectivity, impartiality, and detachment that explanation requires. Readily answering the "why" question when there is no answer available is dehumanizing.

A more human (and humane) response in the face of tragedy and loss is to feel. To genuinely feel for others is no easy task, and even more so in our media-saturated culture. Horrors and tragedies are often spun in a twenty-four-hour news cycle; they become media events that draw attention, interest, and, yes, shock value. But eventually, the news crews move to something else, and what was the primary news story for a week running soon becomes "old news," and so people get bored and forget. When tragedies become media spectacles, it is hard to feel genuinely for others. After so many clips and footage, people become desensitized and so indifferent; the

---

6. That is not to say that such realizations require suffering for them to occur in this life, but certainly one finds a pattern oft-repeated in which the two can be correlated.

overexposure through one lens or perspective has the propensity to become tiresome and belabored over time.

What is being offered through the phrase "to feel" is to be genuinely engaged.[7] In this regard, that which surrounds a person actually stakes a claim in that person's life as one seeks to embrace the world with God's love, a species of love that is full and generative rather than contingent and reactive.[8] Of course, that kind of engagement is destabilizing and risky; it is also impossible to engage the totality of loss and pain that the world suffers from. One person cannot bear it all, but one person can bear some of it—and Christians are called to bear, for their Lord led a life of bearing. The Christian life is one of bearing others' burdens. Such a disposition is agapaic, kenotic, and self-sacrificial; in short, it is Christ-like.[9]

And so, for true engagement to take place, feeling ought to lead to a form of doing. Rather than postulating analyses and theories, Christians ought to be about the business of healing and repairing the world in light of their vision of God's

7. I hope that by offering feeling as an alternative to explanation that I do not mischaracterize the mission of the church as overly sentimental, for sentimentalism is partly responsible for the incoherent thinking that persists in theodical reactions. What I mean by "to feel" is to be compelled by the beauty of the gospel and repulsed by the decay of the world so that in turn one is moved to act toward the world's healing and repair in a gospel-shaped way.

8. Hart references St. Isaac the Syrian here to elaborate this "ecstasy of universal charity": "What is a merciful heart? A heart aflame for all of creation. . . . The heart of such a man is humbled by the powerful and fervent mercy that has captured it and by the immense compassion it feels, and it cannot endure to see or hear of any suffering or any grief anywhere within the creation" (*Doors of the Sea*, 59).

9. I expand on this point in *The Apathetic God*, particularly ch. 6.

in-breaking kingdom.[10] Christians cannot establish this kingdom or cause it to be through their sheer efforts, but they can
proclaim it, and doing so is not simply a verbal activity; rather,
it is a hands-on affair. Binding wounds, mending brokenness,
and meeting needs are at the heart of what it means to be light
in the world and salt of the earth.

One way of categorizing this stance is to say that on offer
in these reflections is a pastoral approach to theodicy. One
of the difficulties with the way church is envisioned in contemporary and "developed" contexts is that the clergy are collectively conceived to be a service-oriented agency toward the
laity. Pastors, priests, and other ecclesial officers are to bear
the burdens of the congregation and to do so largely alone
and in isolation. With such a conception in place, it is no
wonder that loneliness and burnout are at the heart of min-
isterial dissatisfaction and failure. There are simply too many
burdens in a single congregation for a pastoral staff, much less
a single pastor, to carry. Christian community is not meant to
work in such a fashion. As Bonhoeffer remarked, Christian
community (*Gemeinde*) exists with the understanding that
we present Christ one to another.[11] Another way of stating
the matter is that we are to be pastoral to one another. All of
God's people are to shepherd one another and nurture one

10. This gesture is at the heart of John Swinton's call for a "practical
theodicy," which he says "assumes that God is in and for the world, not
in abstract reasoning, but in compassionate actions of resistance and
transformation. [A practical theodicy] does not view the problem of
evil as a dislocated philosophical argument but rather as a grounded
context for practical, faithful engagement with the reality of evil and
human suffering" (*Raging with Compassion*, 86).

11. This theme is a running motif in *Life Together*.

another since the needs are so great and vast within any collective of individuals.

If Christians are to be pastoral to one another, then they have the charge to engage in a number of pastoral practices that may not come naturally to them, but these practices are nonetheless vital if the church is to be the church, both to those within and outside of its walls. One such practice was already alluded to above: the suspension of explanation in favor of bearing one another's burdens and of feeling and walking with others. In a context that operates at such a frenzied pace, stopping to engage one another and to bear one another's burdens is difficult to manage, but it should not be left exclusively to a specialized, psychotherapeutic industry (as helpful as that sector of support is). Engaging one another in a genuine way means living sacrificially and kenotically, taking up that which is not our own for purposes of healing and supporting those in need. Such a *modus operandi* is not so much a strategy as a disposition and approach to the wider world.

In light of this last point, being pastoral to one another means not instrumentalizing or objectifying the other. It is so easy to look at others as charity cases or as projects, but in some ways such approaches de-dignify and dehumanize. People, both inside and outside of the church, are not "things" (causes, souls in need of saving, or some other label); they are God's creatures created in God's image. Humans have names; they have stories and experiences; they have needs and desires, joys and pains. Bearing one another's burdens means delving deep into the common humanity that we all share and affirming that commonality together. None of us is outside of the possibility of feeling lonely, being hungry, suffering pain, or experiencing loss. For that reason, we cannot treat the other as simply a category or a case number. Doing so would be harmful, both to the other and the self.

A final practice worth noting at present is the practice of listening and being with people.[12] Oftentimes, explanations rise to the surface because the "caregiver" wants to fix the problems at hand. In a very speedy and technologically savvy context like ours, such tendencies are easy to cultivate. But certain situations cannot be fixed. People oftentimes do not want to hear that "it's all going to work out," "God has a plan for you," or "I know just what you are going through because something like this happened to me five years ago." There is a certain propriety involved with bearing one another's burdens, meaning that one has to resist the tendency to want to make things more tolerable for all those involved in crisis ministry. It is not fun being in a room where somebody is screaming and crying hysterically or where somebody is yelling at you to explain why God allowed something to happen. It takes a toll on onlookers to see young children watching their parents being buried, or a young mother finding out that her child has a chronic, incurable disease. Such developments obviously hurt those immediately affected, but they also hurt

---

12. Although space constraints limit what can be said here, Frederick W. Schmidt's points regarding the building of a caring community coincide with much of what has been said so far; these include 1) the resistance to claim to "know" what others are experiencing, 2) the resistance to explain away the agony of those who struggle with loss, 3) the avoidance of easy answers, 4) the suspension of rushing one who suffers to closure, 5) the avoidance of weighing the spiritual maturity or worth of those who suffer on the basis of their response, 6) identifying and opposing those causes of suffering that result from human cruelty or callousness, and 7) being present (*When Suffering Persists*, ch. 6).

those alongside of them, making them feel very awkward, out of place, and out of control.

At such moments, people, often out of their need to provide help and comfort to others *and themselves*, say more than they ought and in turn may damage the person exceedingly in the process. This author is of the perspective that no one, in an effort to help the other, should offer such words as "It was his time to go," "It's okay, God needed her at this time," or "Don't worry: God is in control and so this is God's plan." Again, caregivers and supporters often do more damage than comfort by filling the void created by chaos, evil, and pain with platitudinous, nonsensical, and unverifiable claims. Who is to say that God needed the person right now? How can we even know this? Don't we on earth need people? How can we honestly say that it was a person's time to go, especially when one dies as an infant or teenager? How can we genuinely engage one another when we don't allow the other to be angry, sad, or upset when her world has been rocked and shaken to its very foundation?

Often, when these "words of comfort" are offered, people grow increasingly bitter and upset at the church and at God since both are implicated when self-identified Christians seek to help but are, ultimately, out of line. With sensitive situations like the ones alluded to above, good intentions are not enough. All of these considerations show that listening and allowing the other space to be are vital sensibilities to be fostered when evil, pain, sin, suffering, and death come to us.

And it is not a matter of if, but when they come. Living in this fallen world means living side by side with the constant threat of evil, sin, suffering, and death. We all will suffer. Undoubtedly, some seem to suffer more than "their fair share," but all suffer; everyone has to check evil in one's own life, and all will face death at some point. Such sensibilities are not necessarily morbid. They constitute a sobering realism on the basis of how things are.

Yet Christians are called to live in peace, joy, and love. Can we lead meaningful lives in light of the fact that we will all die? Is it possible to recognize beauty and truth in the midst of decay and falsehoods? The challenge of the Christian life is to approach life not as a necessary tragedy but as a promised, hopeful possibility. Christians believe that their lives will end in a blessed manner, that they as God's creatures will pass through death, but do so on their way to meet their Creator. And because this Creator willed to heal and restore all that is, as evidenced by the life, death, and resurrection of Jesus, Christians have all the more reason to be a hopeful people. The creation has a hopeful future because its future is God.

The Christian gospel proclaims that it is not necessary to face evil, sin, suffering, and death in a cowardly fashion. We can face such realities because God has gone on and faced them before us, and he came out of such an encounter as victorious, as Lord, as the giver and restorer of life. With such a hope, Christians, along with the rest of the creation, can only proclaim, "Maranatha!"—"Come, our Lord!"

Bibliography

Adams, Marilyn McCord. *Horrendous Evils and the Goodness of God.* Ithaca: Cornell University Press, 1999.

Bauckham, Richard. "Theodicy from Ivan Karamazov to Moltmann." *Modern Theology* 4 (1987) 83–97.

Bonhoeffer, Dietrich. *Creation and Fall: A Theological Exposition of Genesis 1–3.* Translated by Martin Rüter and Ilse Tödt. Edited by John W. de Gruchy. Dietrich Bonhoeffer Works 3. Minneapolis: Fortress, 1997.

———. *Life Together.* Translated by John W. Doberstein. New York: Harper, 1954.

Boyd, Gregory A. *Satan and the Problem of Evil: Constructing a Trinitarian Warfare Theodicy.* Downers Grove, IL: InterVarsity, 2001.

Brueggemann, Walter. *The Message of the Psalms: A Theological Commentary.* Minneapolis: Augsburg, 1984.

Burrell, David B. *Deconstructing Theodicy: Why Job Has Nothing to Say to the Puzzle of Suffering.* Grand Rapids: Brazos, 2008.

Castelo, Daniel. *The Apathetic God: Exploring the Contemporary Relevance of Divine Impassibility.* Paternoster Theological Monographs. Eugene, OR: Wipf & Stock, 2009.

———. "The Fear of the Lord as Theological Method." *Journal of Theological Interpretation* 2 (2008) 147–60.

Clarke, Samuel. "The Boyle Lectures." In *Deism and Natural Religion: A Source Book*, edited by Graham Waring, 44–55. New York: Frederick Unger, 1967.

Dostoyevsky, Fyodor. *The Brothers Karamazov.* Translated by Richard Pevear and Larissa Volokhonsky. New York: Farrar, Straus & Giroux, 1990.

Duff, Nancy J. "Recovering Lamentation as a Practice of the Church." In *Lament*, edited by Sally A. Brown and Patrick D. Miller, 3–14. Louisville: Westminster John Knox, 2005.

Ehrman, Bart. *God's Problem: How the Bible Fails to Answer Our Most Important Question—Why We Suffer*. New York: HarperOne, 2008.

Emerson, Michael O., and Christian Smith. *Divided by Faith*. Oxford: Oxford University Press, 2000.

Fretheim, Terence E. *Creation Untamed*. Grand Rapids: Baker Academic, 2010.

Gutiérrez, Gustavo. *On Job*. Maryknoll, NY: Orbis, 1987.

Hall, Douglas John. *God and Human Suffering*. Minneapolis: Augsburg, 1986.

Hart, David Bentley. *The Doors of the Sea: Where Was God in the Tsunami?* Grand Rapids: Eerdmans, 2005.

Hauerwas, Stanley. *God, Medicine, and Suffering*. Grand Rapids: Eerdmans, 1990.

Hume, David. *Dialogues concerning Natural Religion*. Cambridge: Cambridge University Press, 2007.

Keating, James F., and Thomas Joseph White, editors. *Divine Impassibility and the Mystery of Human Suffering*. Grand Rapids: Eerdmans, 2009.

Kushner, Harold S. *When Bad Things Happen to Good People*. New York: Avon, 1981.

Leibniz, Gottfried Wilhelm. *Theodicy*. Chicago: Open Court, 1990.

Long, D. Stephen. *The Goodness of God: Theology, Church, and the Social Order*. Grand Rapids: Brazos, 2001.

MacIntyre, Alasdair C., and Paul Ricoeur. *The Religious Significance of Atheism*. New York: Columbia University Press, 1969.

McCabe, Herbert. *God and Evil in the Theology of St. Thomas Aquinas*. New York: Continuum, 2010.

———. *God Matters*. Springfield, IL: Templegate, 1987.

Moltmann, Jürgen. *The Crucified God: The Cross as the Foundation and Criticism of Christian Theology*. Minneapolis: Fortress, 1993.

Officer, Charles, and Jake Page. *When the Planet Rages: Natural Disasters, Global Warming, and the Future of the Earth*. Oxford: Oxford University Press, 2009.

Pagels, Elaine H. *Adam, Eve, and the Serpent*. New York: Random House, 1988.

Pauw, Amy Plantinga. "Dying Well." In *Living Well and Dying Faithfully: Christian Practices for End-of-Life Care*, edited by John Swinton and Richard Payne, 17–29. Grand Rapids: Eerdmans, 2009.

Peck, M. Scott. *People of the Lie: The Hope for Healing Human Evil*. New York: Touchstone, 1983.

Schmidt, Frederick W. *When Suffering Persists: A Theology of Candor*. Harrisburg, PA: Morehouse, 2001.

Surin, Kenneth. "Theodicy?" *Harvard Theological Review* 76 (1983) 225–47.

———. *Theology and the Problem of Evil.* New York: Blackwell, 1986.

Swinton, John. *Raging with Compassion.* Grand Rapids: Eerdmans, 2007.

———. "Why Me, Lord?" In *Living Well and Dying Faithfully: Christian Practices for End-of-Life Care,* edited by John Swinton and Richard Payne, 107–38. Grand Rapids: Eerdmans, 2009.

Tanner, Kathryn. *Jesus, Humanity and the Trinity: A Brief Systematic Theology.* Minneapolis: Fortress, 2001.

Thiel, John E. *God, Evil, and Innocent Suffering: A Theological Reflection.* New York: Herder & Herder, 2002.

Tilley, Terrence W. *The Evils of Theodicy.* Eugene, OR: Wipf & Stock, 2000.

Tindal, Matthew. "Christianity as Old as the Creation." In *Deism and Natural Religion,* edited by Graham Waring, 107–70. New York: Frederick Unger, 1967.

Voltaire. "Author's Preface to the Lisbon Earthquake." In *The Works of Voltaire,* 36:5–7. Chicago: DuMont, 1901.

———. "The Lisbon Earthquake." In *The Works of Voltaire,* 36:8–18. Chicago: DuMont, 1901.

Willis, W. Waite. *Theism, Atheism, and the Doctrine of the Trinity: The Trinitarian of Karl Barth and Jürgen Moltmann in Response to Protest Atheism.* Atlanta: Scholars, 1987.

Wright, N. T. *Evil and the Justice of God.* Downers Grove, IL: InterVarsity, 2006.

Young, Frances M. *Face to Face.* Edinburgh: T. & T. Clark, 1990.